DESPERADOES
OF THE
OZARKS

DESPERADOES
OF THE
OZARKS

LARRY WOOD

PELICAN PUBLISHING COMPANY
Gretna 2011

The word "Pelican" and the depiction of a pelican are
trademarks of Pelican Publishing Company, Inc., and are
registered in the U.S. Patent and Trademark Office.

Library of Congress Cataloging-in-Publication Data

Wood, Larry (Larry E.)
  Desperadoes of the Ozarks / Larry Wood.
      p. cm.
  Includes bibliographical references and index.
  ISBN 978-1-58980-962-8 (pbk. : alk. paper) 1. Ozark
Mountains—History—Anecdotes. 2. Outlaws—Ozark
Mountains—Biography—Anecdotes. 3. Criminals—Ozark
Mountains—Biography—Anecdotes. 4. Crime—Ozark
Mountains—History—Anecdotes. 5. Ozark Mountains—
Biography—Anecdotes. 6. Ozark Mountains—History, Local—
Anecdotes. I. Title.
  F417.O9W659 2011
  976.7'1–dc23
                                        2011034315

Printed in the United States of America

Published by Pelican Publishing Company, Inc.
1000 Burmaster Street, Gretna, Louisiana 70053

Contents

Preface

My previous book on the subject of outlawry in the Ozarks, *Ozarks Gunfights and Other Notorious Incidents,* chronicled twenty-five events that occurred in the region between the close of the Civil War and the middle of the twentieth century. The current work tells the stories of an additional twenty-two. In only one case does a subject appear in both books. The first volume told the story of Bonnie and Clyde's shootout with Joplin, Missouri, police in April of 1933, while this one devotes a chapter to the desperate duo's other notorious shenanigans in the Ozarks.

To anyone who might question whether there were forty-seven incidents and/or characters in the Ozarks from 1865 to 1950 that can rightly be described as notorious, let me just say that I have picked only the most infamous—the ones that have a sensational or at least an unusual element to them. If a man committed a simple murder and was sentenced to life imprisonment for his crime, his story probably didn't make it into either book. However, if he killed a whole string of people, if he was lynched by a mob in retaliation for his crime, or if the crime stood out in some other fashion, I at least took a second look at the story, and it may well have made it into one of the two books. While some of the incidents and characters in this book may not be well known, these tales of true crime are intriguing, as several of them have not been previously told except in newspapers of the period. I hope

you will find the stories of these desperadoes as fascinating as
I have.

Acknowledgments

A number of libraries, museums, and historical groups provided photographs or information for this book, and I would like to recognize those facilities and organizations. They include the Arkansas History Commission, the Baxter Springs Heritage Museum, the Granby Mining Museum, the Historical Museum for Springfield-Greene County, the Jacksonport State Park, the Jasper County Records Center, the Joplin Public Library, the Kansas Historical Society, the Logan County Historical Museum, the Neosho-Newton County Library, the Pleasant Hill Historical Society, the Springfield-Greene County Library, the State Historical Society of Missouri-Columbia, and the Texas County Historical Society.

I also want to thank certain individuals, some associated with the organizations listed above and some not, who helped me with the book in one way or another. They include Phyllis Abbott, Mark Ballard, Jesse Bellard, Linda Childers, Patty Crane, Dixie Haase, Jim Hounschell, Angela Jackson, Bob Kennedy, Lisa Keys, Scott Mallatt, Larry O'Neal, Jeanne Reynolds, Kathy Richardson, R. J. Savage, Earleene Spaulding, Jason Sullivan, and Steve Weldon.

I also want to thank Pelican editor Nina Kooij for her excellent edit of the manuscript. I know the final product is better because of her input.

As is normally the case with my writing, my wife, Gigi,

served as the first reader of many of these stories, and I thank her not only for her proofreading skills but also for her continued support and encouragement.

DESPERADOES
OF THE
OZARKS

1

A Horrible and Fiendish Murder and a Swift and Merited Vengeance

Twenty-year-old Jackson Carney must have been surprised when his wayward cousin, twenty-six-year-old George Moore, showed up one morning at the store Jackson ran with his nineteen-year-old bride of ten months, Cordelia. It was around eleven on Saturday, December 4, 1869, in Shell Knob, Missouri, just west of the Barry-Stone county line. About a year earlier, Jackson's father, John, had sent Moore to escort an old man home from the Carney place north of Shell Knob after the man became too intoxicated to be trusted with his team of horses. But instead of seeing to the man's safety, Moore used the opportunity to rob him of ten dollars and then fled to Arkansas.

Around the first of December, though, Moore had reappeared in Barry County at Gadfly (present-day Corsicana), west of Purdy, and now he was back at Shell Knob. According to the *Springfield Missouri Patriot*, he "exhibited a great deal of pleasure" at seeing his cousin and "made himself very familiar with him." In fact, he was "more familiar than seemed agreeable to Carney," but what was the young storekeeper to do?

After all, George Moore wasn't just a cousin to Jackson Carney; he was more like a brother. Moore had grown up in the Carney home after his own parents died of smallpox when he was a young child. Therefore, despite any misgivings he might have had about his errant cousin's sudden reappearance,

Carney treated Moore "with the considerations due to an old friend." He even scuffled goodnaturedly with the visitor when Moore kept pressing him to do so.

Moore hung around the store throughout the day "with every appearance of friendship between the two young men, but scarcely had the sun gone down," according to the Springfield newspaper, "and the last of the day's visitors left the store, when Moore threw off his disguise, and enacted the bloody and heartless crime" for which he had apparently come. With darkness approaching, Moore shot Jackson Carney once in the mouth and once in the throat. Then he fired a bullet into the young woman's head from such close range that a portion of her clothes caught fire from the blast and burned almost to her waist.

After the murders, Moore promptly struck out about nine miles toward Cassville and spent the night at the home of a man named Lewis Woodridge. On Sunday, the murderer attended church services at the Horner schoolhouse, southeast of Cassville.

Meanwhile, the bodies of his victims were not discovered until about four o'clock on Sunday afternoon, when a customer stopped at the store to pick up some goods he had purchased the day before. Upon entering the unlocked building, the customer found Carney lying on his back in the storeroom. Cordelia was lying about twenty feet away near the living quarters of the double-log structure.

Who could have perpetrated such a horrific crime? Carney's customers remembered that his ornery cousin had hung around the store the previous day. He had been seen there as late as sundown, and a neighbor who lived about a quarter of a mile away said he had heard three shots from the direction of the store shortly after dusk. And now the unlikely visitor was gone, and two dead bodies lay on the storeroom floor! George Moore was immediately suspected of the atrocity, and word was sent to Barry County officers at Cassville to be on the lookout for the fugitive. On Monday morning, December 6, Sheriff John H. Moore (no apparent relation) apprehended young Moore about a mile and a half south of Cassville and took him back to the county jail.

At the time of his arrest, Moore was carrying about two hundred dollars, stashed a little here and a little there in various pockets of his attire. The money was identified as having been taken from Carney's store, because some of it had traces of yellow dye on it. Shortly before her murder, young Mrs. Carney had dyed some woolen material yellow and then handled some bills while her hands were still wet. In addition, the captive was wearing a hat that belonged to Jackson Carney, and he had Carney's revolver strapped to his waist. Moore's own hat and one of his pistols were found back at the scene of the crime. Although Moore denied having committed the slayings, the evidence against him seemed overwhelming.

On Monday evening, a mob of enraged friends and relatives of the murder victims converged on Cassville, intent on taking the law into their own hands. But the sheriff safeguarded the prisoner by secretly whisking him away from the jail and into the countryside.

The next day, Jackson Carney and his wife were buried at the Carney Cemetery (now called the Old Carney Cemetery), on Flat Creek in eastern Barry County. "There were more persons present at this funeral," the editor of the *Cassville Democrat* observed, "than ever assembled at any funeral in this county."

Young Carney's grandfather, Thomas Carney, was one of the earliest settlers of Barry County and had served as a county judge during the 1860s. Jackson's father, John, was a well-respected merchant who operated a store at Flat Creek and, in conjunction with the Springfield firm of Robertson and Mason, had recently opened the Shell Knob branch for his son to run. Jackson himself was well known and well liked throughout the area, and his wife was considered "one of the best of women," according to the *Democrat*. "The neighbors

Jackson and Cordelia Carney double stone at Old Carney Cemetery on Flat Creek in eastern Barry County.

and acquaintances were excited to the very highest extent by this sad occurrence. Nothing but seeing the murderer punished could satisfy them."

On Wednesday, December 8, between one hundred and two hundred friends and neighbors of the victims once again gathered and marched into Cassville shortly before noon, intent on vigilante justice. The sheriff at first thought they had come to town for George Moore's preliminary hearing, which was scheduled for later in the day, since several of them were supposed to appear as witnesses. But when the sheriff informed them that the accused man would, indeed, be accorded due process, they flew into a rage. Nobody had accorded Jackson and Cordelia Carney due process!

The *Cassville Banner* reported that the mob surrounded the sheriff and demanded the keys to the jail, "at the same time enforcing their demand by presenting revolvers." Knowing that he was facing "an enraged . . . and deeply injured people, and that they meant what they said," Sheriff Moore gave up the keys.

George Moore was dragged from the jail and taken to a bell post that stood at the southeast corner of the courthouse square. Several wooden boxes, removed from nearby stores, were set beneath an overhanging arm of the post, and Moore was forced to mount the boxes with a noose around his neck. The other end of the rope was tossed over the horizontal arm of the post. Given an opportunity to confess his crime, Moore instead maintained his innocence. Then someone (reportedly a cousin or brother of Jackson Carney and also a cousin of Moore) kicked a box out from under the prisoner, and he was, as the *Democrat* phrased it, left "hanging suspended in the atmosphere with nothing to sustain him but the hangman's rope." The body dangled from the bell post throughout the afternoon and was finally cut down about sunset and buried in an unmarked grave at the Oak Hill Cemetery at the east edge of Cassville.

Very little, if any, effort was made to identify and bring to justice the members of the mob who lynched Moore. In their report of the incident a week after the fact, the editors of the *Missouri Patriot*, calling the killing of the Carneys "one of the most horrible and fiendish murders that has occurred in this part of the country for many years," seemed to sum up the prevailing attitude toward the vigilante hanging. "The taking of the law out of the hands of those legally authorized to execute it is always to be regretted, and is a dangerous practice; but in a case like this we can easily excuse the anger and indignation which hurried this impious wretch to a swift and merited vengeance."

2

Baxter Springs: First Kansas Cow Town

Before L. B. Wright moved to Baxter Springs, Kansas, in early 1871, he had heard disturbing rumors about the wide-open cow town, and he worried that he would be landing himself in a hellhole of iniquity. His fears didn't miss the mark by much.

What he found was a growing young town pulsing with excitement under the stimulus of a thriving Texas cattle trade. Businesses popped up overnight like fresh shoots of prairie grass, and money flowed like the gushing waters of Spring River skirting the town. During the high tide of the cattle season, the town bustled with activity day and night. Shouting and laughter spilled from the Lone Star Saloon, where thirsty Texas cowboys, fresh off the dusty Shawnee Trail and 100 days in the saddle, dosed themselves with the tonic of whiskey. Sporting women beckoned from bawdy houses and dancehalls, peddling an elixir of a different sort. Gamblers camped in the town's saloons, tapping the free-spending spirit of the rowdy cowpokes. On the plank boards along Military Road, Baxter's main street, strolled outlaws and ruffians of every stripe. Gunplay erupted with alarming regularity, and the hanging tree at the edge of Baxter was occasionally called into service. It didn't take Mr. Wright long to conclude that the town had duly earned its reputation as "an immoral and evil place."

Though less known than some of the booming Kansas

cattle towns like Dodge City that flourished later, Baxter Springs roared just as loudly for a brief time, and it still lays claim to one title the others can't: "First Cow Town in Kansas." In the years immediately preceding the Civil War, when Baxter was a mere outpost, it served as a stopover for cattle driven north along the Shawnee Trail to Sedalia, Missouri, and other markets, and it became the primary destination for herd after herd of Longhorns trailed from Texas in the first year after the war. In 1866, more than 250,000 head of cattle were received at Baxter Springs.

By the following year, Baxter received only about 35,000 head, its status as the primary destination for Texas cattle threatened by competition from towns like Abilene and other factors. The town, though, continued its rapid growth, and in 1868 the cattle trade also recovered somewhat under the promoting hand of the Stockyards and Drovers Association, which was organized to buy and sell cattle. The group built corrals to accommodate 20,000 head with plenty

Street scene of early-day Baxter Springs. (Courtesy Baxter Springs Heritage Museum)

of grazing ground and clean water. Cowboys were therefore relieved of having to tend their herds twenty-four hours a day while in the area. They were free to seek other pastimes, and in the rip-roaring town of Baxter Springs they didn't have to look very hard.

The Christmas celebration of 1869 suggests the raucous tone of affairs in the town. According to one observer, quite a number of people "imbibed pretty freely of Martin's or Cooley's 'best,' and were promenading the streets in high glee, occasionally running against each other, striking heads against fists—drawing revolvers on each other, innocent amusements as characterizes the devotees of 'Bacchus,' and when placed 'hors du combat' by reason of taking too much 'Tea,' or making rather unusual demonstrations in the service of the 'Drunken god' were marched or toted off to the lockup."

About the same time, a clergyman passed through Baxter Springs and found the town agog with excitement over an upcoming horserace. Forced to lay over for two nights and a day, the churchman was shocked by the frenzy of activity surrounding the contest. The stopover itself was bad enough but "was rendered more unpleasant by the abounding wickedness of the people," he told a Memphis newspaper. "I do not think I ever heard as much profanity in twenty-four hours in all my life."

The arrival of the Kansas City, Fort Scott, and Gulf Railroad in the spring of 1870 revived Baxter's flagging cattle trade, and the town flourished along with it. That summer would see eighty carpenters working in Baxter Springs, each with a two-week backlog. The booming cow town was in its heyday, and its riotous, anything-goes reputation was at its peak.

In April of that year, the editor of the town's *Cherokee Sentinel* groused that "houses of ill-fame, gambling hells, keno halls, and faro banks have for some time been under full headway in Baxter." A month later, a newspaperman from neighboring Columbus chimed in disapprovingly, "There is not a church in Baxter Springs. It is filled with gambling hells and lewd women."

In September, a group of prostitutes who were run out of Abilene boarded a train for Baxter Springs, where they presumably received a warmer welcome. Fancy women glutted the city during 1870, working out of saloons and bawdy houses or more often setting up shop in shanties at the edge of town. A police blotter from one month shows thirty-three soiled doves arrested for plying their trade in Baxter. Belle Williams, Mollie Blair, and a host of coworkers were booked for "acts of lewdness," while Sallie Beets and Miss Maud were charged with "running a lewd house." All were fined from six to sixteen dollars and set free to resume their sport.

Although local citizens generally welcomed the cattle business, by the fall of 1870 the revelry of the Texas "roughs" was starting to wear thin among some of the townspeople, and, according to one report, law officers were "compelled to be rather severe in order to maintain the peace." The clampdown created a festering resentment among the cowboys, and on the night of November 7, the Texans' animosity toward local authorities erupted into violence on the main street of Baxter Springs.

Cowpoke Thomas Good was drinking and carousing with a "courtesan" named Nellie Starr at the Wiggins House, a hotel and saloon on the corner of Ninth Street and Military Road, where Nellie was employed. When Mr. Wiggins tried to quiet the loud and boisterous couple, Nellie, a newcomer from Kansas City, became indignant and starting arguing with her employer. The hotelkeeper finally summoned H. C. Seaman, the town marshal, who promptly placed Ms. Starr under arrest.

The marshal had escorted his prisoner outside to Military when she stopped and refused to go any farther. As Marshal Seaman turned to Mr. Wiggins and some other bystanders for help, Good, trailing the scene with a Texas buddy, walked up and "presented" his revolver. Seaman quickly released his hold on Nellie Starr to draw his weapon on the two Texans. As soon as he did, Nellie took out a gun and fired toward the crowd, slightly wounding Wiggins. A sharp exchange of gunfire then ensued between Seaman and the two cowboys, and the marshal fell mortally wounded.

Injured in the shooting, Good made his escape but was arrested the next day at a farmhouse a few miles east of town. Seaman died shortly after he was shot, and he was buried in the city cemetery. Nellie Starr was arrested on a charge of carrying a concealed revolver within the city limits and fined $100. Three days after the killing, the Baxter Springs City Council passed an ordinance cracking down on gambling and prostitution and giving keepers of bawdy houses a week to leave town.

Over the next couple of years, drovers increasingly bypassed Baxter Springs as a destination for their herds, but Baxter's waning cattle trade did not soon dampen its rough-and-tumble spirit. After the marshal's death, Mayor J. R. Boyd appointed Cassius M. Taylor to take Seaman's place, but the two soon became political enemies. Taylor opposed Boyd when the latter ran successfully for reelection, and Boyd retaliated by deliberately instigating trouble for the marshal. In one instance, Boyd reportedly went to the manager of traveling circus, a man named Spalding, and told him not to allow Taylor to arrest anyone at the circus, as Taylor was a dangerous and desperate man. The mayor then went to the marshal and instructed him to arrest Spalding on a charge of selling goods without a license. When Taylor went to make the arrest, Spalding resisted, and a shooting affray resulted in which Spalding was wounded. When Taylor learned the details of the affair, he considered it a "put up" job that the mayor had arranged to try to get him killed, and it embittered him toward Boyd even more.

Marshal Cassius Taylor. (Courtesy Baxter Springs Heritage Museum)

Then in late June of 1872, a local lumber man named Smith tried to collect a small debt from Boyd, but instead of paying, the mayor became indignant and struck the businessman, knocking him to the ground. "This rash deed," according to one newspaper report, "Smith considered rather too much to be borne." Swearing out a warrant for Boyd's arrest, he called on Taylor to serve it, and the marshal was more than ready to oblige. In the meantime, though, the mayor heard about the warrant. On the night of June 29, 1872, he armed himself with a Navy Colt that protruded from his breast pocket and a derringer hidden in his pants pocket, then ambled down Military Road.

Spotting Boyd among the Saturday-night crowd on the main street of Baxter, Taylor told the mayor he was under arrest and read the warrant. "Come along," the marshal said.

"All right," Boyd agreed, but as he started down the street with the marshal, he boldly fingered the butt of the Colt.

"I'll need your weapon," Taylor insisted when he saw the defiant gesture.

"Not by a damn sight!" Boyd cried. As the marshal started to take the Colt, the mayor reached into his pants pocket, pulled out the little hideout gun, and shot Taylor once in the chest. The marshal collapsed and died almost immediately.

Boyd tossed the derringer into the street, pulled out his revolver, and strolled down Military. He sought shelter in DeBoice's store among friends, but soon a mob formed and clamored for "Judge Lynch." One of Boyd's friends telegraphed to Columbus for the sheriff to come at once and take Boyd into protective custody. Sheriff James Ludlow arrived in the wee hours of Sunday morning and whisked Boyd away to Columbus, where a few days later, according to friends of the dead marshal, the mayor was "walking around at his leisure, smoking cigars." Boyd was later tried and acquitted for the killing of Taylor, a verdict that further enraged friends of the deceased lawman.

Baxter's cattle trade continued to decline over the next

several years, but the town remained a magnet for lawlessness awhile longer. On April 19, 1876, the Baxter National Bank was robbed, according to local legend, by Jesse James and a companion named Cole who was presumed to be Cole Younger. (Most historians now discount this report, as Jesse and Cole were thought to be elsewhere at the time. Younger gang members Bill Chadwell and Charlie Pitts, who were known to be in the general area of Baxter Springs during the spring of 1876, were the most likely culprits.) The two desperadoes strode into the bank about eleven o'clock and asked cashier H. R. Crowell to change a five-dollar bill. When he turned to complete the transaction, the outlaws pulled out their six-guns, handed him a bag, and ordered him to fill it. After he complied, the robbers herded three bystanders into the bank vault and locked it, then forced the cashier to accompany them to their horses. They mounted up and mockingly suggested that he call for help. The two bandits then rode out of town toward the Indian Nation with $2,900 in newly acquired riches. When news of the robbery reached neighboring Columbus, it was reported that almost $30,000 had been stolen. After the estimate was corrected to $3,000, the editor of the *Columbus Courier* commented wryly, "We trust for the sake of a good sensation, they won't get it any lower."

By this time, only about eight hundred souls populated Baxter, and the town's debt exceeded the assessed value of all its property. When the cattle business was diverted to points farther west and lead was discovered to the east near the Missouri state line, the town's gamblers and other adventurers moved on, leaving just a few steady, year-round residents to shoulder the debt. Building the town into a stable community was left to citizens such as L. B. Wright, who had concluded after a year's residence that Baxter Springs, despite its dubious reputation, was an excellent place to raise a family and "the most charming location in the Southwest."

Unlike Abilene and Dodge City, Baxter Springs has never seen its history popularized in dime novels or Western movies, perhaps because the town lacked a legendary figure like Wyatt Earp or maybe because its heyday as a wild cow town simply came and went too soon. For a number of years during the late nineteenth century, the lack of attention was just fine with its citizens, who were quite willing to forget the town's shady past, but more recently, citizens have embraced the legacy with pride. "Cowtown Days," an annual celebration commemorating the town's early history, was popular for many years during the late 1900s and early 2000s, and billboards along the main roads leading into the community prominently proclaim Baxter's heritage as the "First Cowtown in Kansas."

3

The Notorious Bud Blount:
They Didn't Know Who They
Were Foolin' With

When Allen "Bud" Blount (often spelled Blunt) got into a barroom brawl with George McDonald at the Tip Top mining camp in Arizona Territory on May 25, 1881, Blount tried to warn the man to leave him alone. "You don't know who you're foolin' with," he said ominously. But McDonald hit and wrestled him until Blount broke away, retrieved a pistol from an adjoining room, and fired two fatal shots into the man's body. George McDonald was not the first person who failed to recognize the desperate character of Bud Blount, and he would not be the last to pay dearly for the oversight.

Blount was born around 1850 at Poplar Bluff, in Butler County, Missouri. The family, including three brothers and a sister and parents Jacob and Esther, moved to Bourbon County, Kansas, around 1860 but stayed there only briefly before settling at Granby, Missouri, where a second sister was born. When the Civil War broke out, Jacob Blount, who had been a county clerk back in Poplar Bluff, joined the Confederate army and was killed during the conflict. His sons grew up without a father among the rough characters who infested the booming mining camp of Granby.

Bud, who was also sometimes called "Newt," and older brother John became miners themselves during their youth. Both, especially Bud, quickly developed reputations as reckless young men because of incidents like the one that happened in October of 1870. A man named Johnson passed through Granby headed for Arkansas with a span of fine horses, but another man claiming to be the rightful owner of the animals showed up shortly afterward. He said the horses had been stolen from him, and he secured the services of Bud Blount and Albert Carey for their return. The pair went in pursuit of the horse thief and overtook him near Huntsville, Arkansas. According to the story they told after they got back to Granby, when they ordered the rustler to stop, he jumped from his horse and started firing at them. When they returned fire, the noisy commotion frightened the stolen horses so much that they ran over the thief, trampling him to death. "We do not vouch for the truth of this statement," a Neosho newspaperman commented wryly at the time, "but the boys got back safe—and brought the horses with them."

Three years later, on the night of December 6, 1873, Bud Blount and an acquaintance named John Cole left a saloon in Granby and were strolling unarmed down the dark street when a blaze of gunfire suddenly erupted, knocking Cole to the ground. Blount escaped injury by running around the corner of a building and hiding behind a livery stable for some time before heading home to get his gun. In a later statement, corroborated by Cole's dying declaration, Blount said he had seen two or three shadowy figures on the other side of the gunfire and heard one of them shout, "Shoot him again!"

Albert Carey (who had recently been made city marshal of Granby), Carey's brother Hobbs (who later rode with the James-Younger gang during the Otterville train robbery), and a third man named Daniel Roten were suspected of the crime, but a preliminary hearing failed to produce enough evidence to bring an indictment. The fact that Bud Blount's old pal Albert Carey was one of the main suspects may have contributed to the skepticism the editor of the *Granby Miner* evinced in his report of the bloody deed a week later. Although the newspaperman declined to discuss "all the supposed causes of this foul murder," he said that it seemed "almost a miracle that Blount was not killed, and that no other person was hit." He suggested that the whole incident was "shrouded in a mystery." Whether Blount was somehow in cahoots with Cole's assailants, as the editor seemed to imply, is unclear. Blount was, in fact, indicted in Newton County Circuit Court for felonious assault two months later, but it's not known whether the charge was connected to the killing of Cole.

As suggested by Albert Carey's status as the first city marshal of Granby, the line separating the lawless element from law-abiding citizens was thin during the town's early days. Such a pattern continued in the spring of 1874. Carey had resigned or been removed from the job, and Bud Blount ran unsuccessfully for the post as the candidate of the Workingman's Party. Later the same year, Bud's pal George Hudson, who eventually proved to be an even more desperate character than Bud, began his sporadic service as a deputy marshal under his father, City Marshal C. C. Hudson. Meanwhile, Bud's brother John was involved in a couple of high-stakes horseraces in Granby. Later Bud was indicted in Newton County for gambling, but again it's unclear as to whether the charge was in connection to his brother's horseracing.

In early 1875, the entire Blount family packed up and moved to Arizona Territory, but by late 1876 they were back in Missouri, settling this time at Carterville, a new lead-mining camp that had sprung up twenty miles northwest of their old home at Granby. Some of the Blounts' old buddies from Granby, including George Hudson, joined them at the booming camp.

On January 16, 1877, James Messick, a pal of Blount and Hudson, got himself arrested and incarcerated for drunkenness and disorderly conduct in Webb City, another mining town about a mile west of Carterville. Upon hearing the news, the Blount gang rode over to try to get him released. The effort failed, and they took out their frustration by firing several shots into the jailhouse as they rode off.

Messick paid a fine and was released on the morning of the eighteenth. After he came back to Carterville, the

rowdy gang got tanked up on liquor and decided they
wanted revenge. They galloped into Webb City and started
terrorizing the town. Hudson entered the Scott residence,
followed by the rest of the gang, and commenced to harass a
young woman. When Mr. Scott's young son tried to intervene,
Hudson slapped and threatened the boy, and the lad's father
got off his sickbed and came to the defense of the boy and
the girl. Hudson struck the man in the head with a pistol,
knocking him to the floor. Bud Blount, in the unlikely role
of mediator, stepped in to restrain Hudson, and the drunken
crew then stomped out, saddled up, and rode out of town.

The city marshal and his posse went out looking for the
gang and soon ran onto John Blount near the outskirts of
town. When they tried to arrest him, he opened fire on the
lawmen and made his escape amid a hail of return buckshot
that wounded him in the shoulder and hip.

John rendezvoused with the rest of the gang in Carterville,
and after tending to his injuries, he and the boys headed
back to Webb City late in the afternoon of January 18 armed
with Spencer rifles and carbines for an all-out assault on
the town. They galloped up and down the street shooting
indiscriminately at livestock and citizens, who possessed only
shotguns to defend themselves against the high-powered
rifles. The gang fired an estimated two hundred shots during
the melee, killing a couple of animals and wounding at least
five citizens (although no one was killed), before exhausting
their ammunition and making their escape uninjured.

The gang members were charged with felonious assault,
and the disturbance became locally infamous as "the Webb City
riot" or "the Blunt raid." The Blounts' younger brother Jake was
one of several people rounded up and indicted as accessories
to the crime, although he promptly gave bond and went free.
At one point, even Bud's sisters were subpoenaed as witnesses.
The older Blount boys, though, remained on the loose.

Their sidekick George Hudson, who was under indictment
for an earlier murder charge, was handed over by his

bondsmen to a deputy sheriff at Granby in early April. One of the Blounts (presumably Bud) helped him escape, though, by slipping him a pistol when he stepped outside the saloon where the deputy and bondsmen were enjoying a drink.

About this same time, Bud Blount and other members of the gang teamed up briefly with Jake Killian, another tough from Granby who had just been released from the state prison after serving three and half years for the murder of traveling-circus owner William Lake. Killian, who was at least ten years older than Bud, led the gang into Pierce City, where, according to a later newspaper report, they tried to take over the town but "got too drunk to do it."

Sometime during the latter part of 1877, the Blount brothers and George Hudson decided to get away from southwest Missouri. They moved to the mining town of Leadville, Colorado, and soon resumed their criminal careers. In early June of 1879 near Granite, about seventeen miles south of Leadville, they killed one man and waylaid another named Henry Shultz, bashed him in the head, and robbed him of over $1,500. According to Bud Blount's own testimony years later, he and Hudson also killed a lawman at Leadville around the same time.

Shortly after these incidents, Bud headed for Arizona Territory and the Silver Belt mine near Prescott, where the family had lived briefly a few years earlier. Meanwhile, his brother John stayed in Leadville, while his mother and one sister went back to Missouri (as did George Hudson). In the spring of 1881, Bud moved to Tip Top, another mining community, about fifty miles south of Prescott.

On May 24, he was drinking in a saloon and heard another miner named George McDonald cursing about a mutual acquaintance. Blount relayed news of the insults to the third man, and the next day McDonald came looking for him for having betrayed a confidence. He found Blount in Bostwick's saloon and started cursing, grabbing, and shoving him. "Let me go," Blount warned. "You don't know who you are foolin' with."

Wyatt Earp, who helped get Bud Blount released from prison. (Courtesy Arizona Historical Society/Tucson)

The pair grappled briefly before Blount broke loose and strode into a backroom, where he armed himself with a pistol. "The damned son of a bitch!" he swore as he returned to confront McDonald. He fired a shot over his assailant's head and struck him on the side of the face, and when McDonald kept fighting, he fired two shots into the man's body, killing him almost instantly.

Blount fled the scene, but he was chased down, arrested by the county sheriff, and charged with murder. In a trial that ended on June 18, he was found guilty of a lesser charge of manslaughter and sentenced to five years in the Arizona Territorial Prison. Shortly afterward, a man calling himself Jack Johnson arrived in Tombstone and offered his services to Wyatt Earp as a gunman and an informant against Earp's enemies in exchange for Earp's help in getting Bud Blount released from prison. Earp had heard of the Blount brothers, and he believed that Jack Johnson was really Bud's brother John. Feeling that Bud Blount was "about half way right" in his claim of self-defense, Earp interceded on Bud's behalf and helped get him pardoned and released on March 11, 1883.

According to later reports, Bud Blount spent some time in New Mexico after his release from the Arizona prison, but he was back in his old home territory of southwest Missouri within a year or so. On May 14, 1884, he was arrested in possession of a pair of stolen mules near Ritchey, Missouri, about five miles northeast of Granby, after being overtaken there by the animals' owners, who had trailed the thief all the way from Batesville, Arkansas. Blount was lodged temporarily in the county jail at Neosho to await the action of a grand jury. Noting that "Bud Blunt is wanted in several places," a local newspaperman speculated that the thief would be returned to Arkansas, but he was instead sent to Kansas to face charges of horse stealing in Montgomery County. At Pierce City, some of Blount's brutish pals boarded the train that was carrying him to Kansas as though to attempt a rescue, but they dropped off at Sarcoxie after finding the prisoner heavily guarded.

Blount was convicted of grand larceny and sentenced to six years in the Kansas State Penitentiary at Lansing. When he was received at the prison on August 4, 1884, he gave his age as thirty-four, his occupation as smelter, and his marital status as single. He was listed as five feet eight inches tall with a light complexion, light hair, and blue eyes, and he signed his name "Bud Blount."

Blount was released in March of 1890, having served almost the full six years to which he was sentenced. He moved back to Carterville, where his mother and sister lived, and began running a gambling house. On December 26, 1890, he visited his old hometown of Granby, and when he got ready late that afternoon to board the train that would take him back home to Carterville by way of Pierce City, he was asked by brakeman Jack Majors to wait until the disembarking passengers got off before boarding. Later, after boarding the train, Blount started grumbling that he "would like to find the son of a bitch that would object to me getting on this train when and as I pleased."

After taking a seat in the ladies' car, Blount pulled out a whiskey bottle and began drinking from it. Conductor John Gillies told Blount he should go to the smoking car if he wanted to drink. Blount refused and became belligerent, waving a knife at Gillies, but he finally followed the conductor outside to a platform between cars. When Majors happened along and seized Blount by the arm to try to coax him toward the smoking car, Blount pulled out a Smith and Wesson .38 caliber revolver. He shot the brakeman twice, in the face and neck, severing his jugular vein and splattering the nearby Gillies with blood. As Majors collapsed mortally wounded, Blount turned the weapon toward Gillies and fired a shot that grazed the conductor's neck. Apparently thinking, because of all the blood on Gillies's face, that he was seriously wounded, too, Blount momentarily let down his guard, and the conductor quickly shoved him off the train as it approached Ritchey.

The train stopped when it reached the village, and a posse immediately went back in search of Blount. They found him near where Gillies had shoved him off, stupefied from a combination of liquor and his fall from the train. The prisoner was hauled back to Ritchey, and the Newton County sheriff arrived shortly afterward and took him to Neosho to await examination. He was indicted for first-degree murder and, following a change of venue from Newton, convicted in early August of 1891 during a trial held at Pineville in McDonald County. Sentenced to hang on September 25, 1891, he was taken back to Neosho to await the execution.

On appeal to the Missouri Supreme Court, though, Blount received a stay of execution until the court could consider the case. In late May of 1892, the high court affirmed the death penalty, but in July the hanging was postponed a second time by gubernatorial edict. Blount finally escaped the death penalty altogether when Missouri governor David Francis commuted his sentence to life imprisonment on September 14, 1892, two days before he was scheduled to die.

The governor's decision was met with disapprobation in southwest Missouri. The editor of the *Joplin Sunday Herald*, for instance, said the only possible mitigating circumstance in the case was Blount's drunkenness, and he suggested that the real reason the convict had escaped the gallows was that he had turned state's evidence against his old pal George Hudson. His testimony had led to a warrant for Hudson's arrest for the assault on Schultz in Colorado over ten years earlier, had ultimately led to Hudson's killing by a deputy sent out to execute the warrant, and had caused the demise of Hudson's gang.

Three days after the commutation of his sentence, Blount began what a local newspaper called his "last excursion." A train took him to the state prison in Jefferson City on September 17, 1892, stopping briefly in Webb City, where his mother and sister met him at the station to say goodbye.

The trip to the state pen, though, turned out not to be

Blount's last excursion after all. On June 28, 1899, Gov. Lawrence Stephens commuted Bud's life sentence to time served, and he was released on July 4, 1899, having logged only six years, nine months, and twenty-one days. Upon his release, he came back to Newton County and lived with his mother at Neosho. Later he became a bartender in nearby Joplin.

In 1902, several citizens of Joplin petitioned Gov. Alexander Dockery for a full pardon for Blount and a restoration of his citizenship. Two of the petitioners, Gilbert Barbee (who had been a witness for the prosecution at the murder trial of Blount's old sidekick George Hudson) and Hugh Dobbs, wrote a letter dated October 3, 1902, testifying that Blount had been a law-abiding, peaceful citizen since his release three years earlier. They claimed that Governor Stephens had agreed to pardon Blount when he commuted his sentence but had neglected to do so. They added that Blount was "a good Democrat" and that they would like for his disabilities to be removed so that he could vote in the upcoming election. Whether politics played a part in the decision is unknown, but Democratic governor Dockery issued the requested pardon on October 7, 1902, just four days after the letter was written.

In his old age, Bud Blount was committed by his sister to the state hospital at Nevada, Missouri, and he died there on March 4, 1928.

4

George Hudson:
Autocrat on the Criminal Throne

When Colorado law officer William Rabedew arrived in Joplin, Missouri, on August 6, 1892, with a warrant for the arrest of George Hudson of neighboring Granby, Joplin policeman Carl Stout knew that serving the writ wouldn't be easy. Hudson was known to have killed five men in four separate incidents and was rumored to have killed several more. Numerous lesser crimes were also attributed to him and his family, but in the rip-roaring mining town of Granby, Hudson, as a Joplin newspaperman suggested, sat on a "criminal throne" and "ruled with a rod of iron." Few people had the temerity to oppose him.

The Hudsons came to Granby from Mississippi around 1868, having left their former home under a cloud of suspicion. George's father, C. C. Hudson, had been a sheriff and was rumored to have embezzled funds, while George was said to have killed an ex-slave when he was just a lad of about fourteen. The family found a home, though, in the wide-open town of Granby. The father was appointed city marshal in 1874, and George and his brothers served as part-time deputies. About the same time that George went to work as a deputy, though, he also went to work on the other side of the law. He was charged in Newton County around the beginning of 1874 with an unknown offense, but the case was nol-prossed in February of that year.

Then in the spring of 1875, a shoemaker named H. H.

Boyensen repaired a pair of boots for George Hudson, and when Hudson returned for them, Boyensen demanded payment before the boots left the shop. During the quarrel that ensued, Hudson shot Boyensen in the leg, and he was subsequently indicted for assault. On the evening of April 14, while he was awaiting trial, Hudson, two of his brothers, and one other man called at Boyensen's home to try to intimidate the shoemaker into not testifying, but Boyensen wouldn't scare. So he was gunned down with a load of buckshot.

Robert Hudson was indicted for murder, and George Hudson, Jack Hudson, and Nathan Tabor were charged as accessories. However, the case was eventually dismissed after the Hudsons reportedly intimidated or drove away the witnesses.

During the wee hours of the morning of October 30, 1875, a man named John Hulsey tried to break into George Hudson's home. After Hudson ordered him to leave, Hulsey kept trying to gain entry, and Hudson shot him dead. At

Jack Hudson, far left, and George Hudson, next to his brother, pose with other men in front of a Granby saloon. (Courtesy Granby Mining Museum)

least one report claimed that Hulsey was a "deaf and dumb mute" who had gone to the wrong house by mistake and was unable to hear Hudson's warning, but the killing was ruled accidental and no charges were filed.

Hudson, his sidekick Bud Blount, and several other men rode into Webb City, about twenty miles northwest of Granby, on January 18, 1877, and started shooting up the town after one of the gang's friends was incarcerated there for public drunkenness. Hudson fired a shot that wounded a bystander named Uriah Fishburn. Although no one was killed, several other men on the street were also wounded, and the incident became known as "the Webb City riot."

Hudson and the other gang members were indicted in Jasper County Court for felonious assault, but Hudson was also still under indictment in Newton County for the Boyensen murder. Turned over by his bondsmen to a Newton County deputy sheriff at Granby in early April of 1877, he made his escape with the help of one of the Blount boys (presumably Bud) before the lawman could get him back to Neosho.

Soon afterward, Hudson took his wife and two young kids and headed for Colorado with Blount, where the pair promptly resumed their criminal careers. In June 1879 they waylaid a man named Shultz at GranitePass, robbed him of $1,700, and left him for dead. During the pair's sojourn in Colorado, according to Blount's later testimony, they also shot and killed a lawman at Leadville, among other lesser crimes.

When Hudson returned briefly to the Ozarks in late 1879, the Jasper County warrant against him for felonious assault was revived, but Hudson didn't hang around long enough for it to be served. On Friday night, November 7, 1879, he, his brother Jack, and Bob Layton were passing through Batesville, Arkansas, with a team of horses (that they had likely stolen) and soon got into a barroom brawl. During the melee, they hit one man over the head with a pistol and fired a shot at another. A posse followed them to their camp just outside town, exchanged shots with them, and captured

George Hudson, but his partners escaped. The next night Layton went back into Batesville to try to break Hudson out of jail. Recognized, Layton was called upon to halt and was shot dead when he went for his gun instead. (Layton and some other men from Granby had killed a man named William "Tiger Bill" St. Clair at Galena, Kansas, on June 16, 1877, but it's not known whether George Hudson was one of the gang. See chapter 6.)

After being bailed out at Batesville in mid-November of 1879 on a $1,500 bond, Hudson went back to Colorado but then returned to Missouri in the early 1880s. Still facing charges for his part in the Webb City riot, he gave bond and went free but soon got involved in another affray at Granby.

On the late afternoon of May 28, 1884, Hudson accosted John Goodykoontz on Main Street in front of Sweet's general store and demanded that Goodykoontz, former postmaster of the Granby post office, stop spreading rumors that the Hudsons had broken into the post office and robbed the safe. The two men argued, and Hudson slapped Goodykoontz on the side of the head.

Nathan Tabor arrived on the scene with his pistol drawn and took Goodykoontz's side in the dispute. (This was the same man who had been indicted with Hudson nine years earlier for the Boyensen murder, but the two were no longer on good terms, partly no doubt because Tabor, acting as a Newton County deputy sheriff, had recently helped in the arrest and extradition to Kansas of Hudson's pal Bud Blount.) City Marshal Hudson hurried from across the street and got between his son and Goodykoontz, but the quarrel escalated. George Hudson said that Tabor and Goodykoontz themselves were the ones who had robbed the post office, and Tabor replied, "You are a damn liar!" Speaking of the Hudsons, Goodykoontz added, "The whole godd— outfit is a set of thieves."

C. C. Hudson persuaded Tabor to put away his gun and then shoved Goodykoontz into the store. Tabor again brandished his revolver as he and George Hudson followed the other two men in. George Hudson pulled his out, too, and bullets started flying, with each man wounding the other. Tabor staggered back outside, and Hudson shot him twice more, including a bullet through the head after Tabor was down. Goodykoontz ran out of the building, but George Hudson shot him dead as he tried to get away.

At Hudson's double-murder trial in November of 1885, conflicting evidence was offered as to who had fired the first shot, and more than one witness said Goodykoontz was unarmed, insinuating that his weapon was planted by Marshal Hudson after the fact. Enough witnesses to get George Hudson acquitted, though, claimed that Tabor had fired first and that Goodykoontz had also fired shots.

Less than a year later, Hudson graduated to murder for hire, gunning down Dr. L. G. Houard without provocation on the evening of September 13, 1886, as the dentist strolled down Main Street in Joplin near the intersection of Third Street. Hudson was finally arrested for the crime in June of 1891, and after a change of venue, the case was heard at Rolla, Missouri, in February of 1892. The evidence presented against Hudson seemed overwhelming. Gilbert Barbee, a prominent Joplin resident who had formerly lived in Granby and had known Hudson for years, was among several witnesses who testified that Peter E. Blow, manager of the Granby Mining Company, had paid Hudson to kill Houard because the latter was romancing Blow's wife. In addition, Barbee and two other former Granby residents, Joe Sittler and Sam Farris, testified that Hudson had tried to sublet the murder contract to Farris. The latter claimed that Hudson said he had "done about all the killing that had been done and that he would be suspected if he did the job." Farris added that Hudson had cursed him and called him a cowardly cur after Farris declined the offer. Despite such damning testimony, Hudson was acquitted in what many observers considered a "bought verdict."

William Rabedew, lawman who killed George Hudson.
(Courtesy Granby Mining Museum)

A few months later, George Hudson was up to his old tricks of intimidating those who dared to oppose him when he and his brother Jack encountered Barbee and Sittler at a Neosho saloon. George slapped Sittler on both sides of his face and chased the two men out of the saloon with a string of threats.

What Hudson hadn't counted on, though, was that his old partner, Bud Blount, would turn against him. In jail awaiting execution for the murder of a railroad brakeman, Blount started talking because he was angry with Hudson for not having offered him more help in his legal defense. Using the information supplied by Blount, those who wanted to rid the country of Hudson decided their best option was to turn to the Colorado authorities. Shultz, the man whom Hudson and Blount had waylaid in Colorado, was located, and he confirmed Blount's story. The warrant for Hudson's arrest was issued, and Rabedew was dispatched to Missouri to bring the fugitive back to Colorado.

Presented with the warrant, Stout, the Joplin policeman, gathered a posse of four men in addition to himself and Rabedew, and the group set out for Granby on the evening of August 6. Once there, the deputies broke into pairs to try to locate Hudson. It was near midnight when Stout and Rabedew finally found him at his saloon, getting ready to close for the night. When Stout told Hudson he was under arrest, George replied, "Not by a damn sight!" and swung a beer bottle at him. Hudson went for his revolver as Stout ducked away, and Rabedew fired a single shot that crashed through Hudson's brain.

"The Killer Killed!" a headline from a Joplin newspaper proudly proclaimed a week later. A Neosho newspaper compared the Hudsons to more infamous Missouri outlaws, such as the Youngers and Jameses. Today, though, memory of the "autocrat" who once sat on the criminal throne in Granby has faded until Hudson is barely a footnote in the local lore of southwest Missouri.

5

A Fatal Affray in Douglas County

When I first read of the March 8, 1879, encounter in Douglas County, Missouri, that left H. H. Vickery, James Shelton "Shelt" Alsup, and Alsup's five-year-old daughter dead, I wondered what could possibly have led to a fatal shootout between a sheriff and ex-sheriff of the same county. Don't lawmen and former lawmen normally cooperate with each other instead of trying to kill each other?

However, things weren't normal in Missouri during the Civil War or for a long time afterward. Bitter divisions created by the war often lingered, making enemies of people who might otherwise have been allies. To fully understand many of the violent episodes that characterized the state during the latter part of the 1800s, one often needs to go all the way back to the war, and so I found it to be with the Alsup-Vickery shootout. If I had been a little more familiar with the territory where this violent incident occurred, I shouldn't have been surprised by it, because nowhere in Missouri was the rancor left over from the war rawer, and nowhere did it linger longer than in Douglas County.

The Alsup family came to the Douglas County area shortly before Shelt was born in 1844. Although the father, Moses Lock Alsup, was a native of Tennessee, the Alsups were strong Union supporters, and after the Civil War broke out, Shelt, his father, three brothers, and an uncle all joined the Union army as members of the Douglas County Home Guard. Later,

Lock, as he was usually called, was made a captain of Company
H, Forty-sixth Regiment Missouri Infantry, and his brother
William was first lieutenant, while his sons served as privates
in the same unit. Benjamin Alsup, another brother to Lock,
lived in Howell County, where he, too, was a strong Union
supporter. During the war, he was captured by Confederates
and held as a prisoner in Arkansas for over three years.

Although Missouri remained in the Union and was under
official Union control for most of the Civil War, the rural
areas of the deeply divided state swarmed with Southern-
allied guerrillas throughout the conflict. One of the primary
duties of Federals stationed in Missouri was hunting down
Confederate bushwhackers and trying to eradicate them
from the state. The Alsups were particularly adept at the
mission and made a name for themselves tracking down and
fighting guerrillas.

The *Official Records of the Union and Confederate Armies*
suggest the nature of the Alsups' reputation. A Union scout
stationed at Rolla reconnoitered through southern Missouri
and into northern Arkansas during the summer of 1863 and
filed a report of his expedition upon his return. "I heard
it stated by several parties," the scout wrote, "that Monks,
Allsop [*sic*] and two sons were doing more harm to their [the
rebel] cause than any other parties, and that men were on
the lookout to shoot them wherever they could find them."
Then, in February of 1865, William N. Alsup filed a report of
his expedition from Douglas County into northern Arkansas.
At Tolbert's Mill on Bennett's River, "we found one guerrilla
or bushwhacker, who we succeeded in killing, and being
satisfied that the mill was a resort of rebels and guerrillas, I
ordered it burned," said Lieutenant Alsup. "I also succeeded
in killing one other guerrilla near the same place."

The lawlessness that characterized the rural areas of
Missouri during the Civil War persisted in some counties
after the conflict was over, and the Alsups joined William
Monks (the Union officer mentioned above) and others,

at the behest of the governor, in helping to reestablish civil law. In some cases, Monks and the Alsups even roamed into northern Arkansas to squash lawless bands, and they sometimes resorted to heavy-handed methods.

These efforts to establish civil law only added to the resentment that ex-Confederates and Southern sympathizers felt toward the Alsups. Most former Confederates were peaceful citizens who didn't condone the unruly bands, but, already disenfranchised by the Drake Constitution of 1865 (which said that no one who had ever been in the Confederate army or sympathized with the Southern cause could vote, run for office, or hold certain jobs such as teacher and preacher without first taking an oath of allegiance), they still resented civil law being imposed by former Federal soldiers, especially when the ex-Union men were outsiders from another county or even another state.

Douglas County, where Lock Alsup became a county officer, was relatively free of ex-bushwhacker bands only because the Alsups ruled the county with an iron fist that alienated even some conservative Union men. Many stories have been handed down in local lore of clashes between the Alsups and other families in the county. No doubt most of the stories contain elements of truth, but it is almost certainly true also that some of them have been exaggerated in the retelling.

One story that is fairly well documented by contemporary sources is the feud between the Alsups and John Hatfield. The thirty-seven-year-old Hatfield settled in the Denlow neighborhood in the northeast part of Douglas County (the same area where the Alsups lived) around 1866 while he was still under indictment in Arkansas for stealing. He was acquitted, soon afterward married a local widow named Elizabeth Davis, and settled down to what he probably anticipated would be a peaceable life of farming. It was not to be, however. Almost from the time Hatfield came to Douglas County, he and the Alsups were at odds. One version of the story suggests that jealousy played a role in the animosity, because one of the Alsups had been somewhat taken with Mrs. Davis before she became involved with Hatfield. Other contributing factors that have been suggested for the ill feeling include "disputed ownership of a horse of surreptitious importation" and Hatfield's refusal to sell a parcel of his new wife's land to one of the Alsups. The main reason for the discord, however, appears to be that Hatfield, although he had served in the Union army throughout the Civil War, was simply "not radical enough for them," as Hatfield himself later explained.

The ill feeling came to a head on September 11, 1870, when a posse of about thirty men led by Judge Lock Alsup and Sheriff William Breazeale called at the Hatfield home to assess and collect county taxes. While the group was there, Hatfield's hired hand, eighteen-year-old Elisha Kincade, got into a dispute with a twenty-three-year-old neighbor named James Cooper and killed him with a knife. According to the Alsups' version of the story, Hatfield immediately took refuge in his house, casting suspicion upon himself as a probable accomplice in the affair. Lock Alsup told the sheriff to arrest Hatfield, and this was quickly accomplished.

Meanwhile, part of the posse pursued Kincade for almost thirty-five miles, caught him, and brought him back to Douglas County. He testified that there had been a disagreement between his boss and Cooper and that Hatfield had instructed him to kill Cooper. Hatfield was turned loose after twenty-four hours, however, with no charges brought against him. He then went to a justice of the peace and swore out warrants against all of the members of the posse who had arrested him, charging them with assault for his rough treatment.

Shortly afterward, with the Alsup band threatening to cut his throat and burn down his house, Hatfield took refuge in nearby Webster County, returning home only clandestinely. While in exile, Hatfield let it be known that he intended to petition Missouri governor B. Gratz Brown to send the state militia to Douglas County. Meanwhile, the assault charges against the posse members were dropped because, according to the Alsup version of the story, the plaintiff did not appear in court on the appointed day or because, according to Hatfield, the sheriff failed to serve the warrants. Whatever the reason, word was sent to Hatfield at Marshfield that he could safely return home.

But then on December 24, 1870, a band of men led by Shelt Alsup was passing by the Hatfield residence when another disturbance broke out. Hatfield claimed that the "posse" fired at least four shots into his house while his family was present, and he implied that they did so without provocation. He also said that they shouted taunts at him, daring "the rebel Brown to send his godd— rebel militia down." (Governor Brown was an ex-Union officer and a former Radical Republican. But prior to the fall election, he had shifted allegiance to the Liberal Republican party, the platform of which included full amnesty for ex-Confederates and the restoration of all their rights.)

Shelt Alsup's version of the Christmas Eve incident was, not surprisingly, quite different from Hatfield's. Alsup said that he only returned fire after Hatfield fired first.

At any rate, Hatfield once again took refuge in Marshfield, from where he wrote an indignant letter to Governor Brown petitioning the state to send militia to Douglas County to restore law and order and asking that Sheriff Breazeale be replaced with a man who would uphold the law fairly for all citizens. Several of the Douglas County citizens who had signed the petition, like Hatfield, had been run out of the county by the Alsups. A few citizens swore out separate affidavits supporting Hatfield's petition and forwarded them to the governor. About the same time that Hatfield sent his letter to the governor, he sent a similar letter to the *St. Louis Times*, and it was published in the newspaper's January 19, 1871, issue under the headline "Outrages by Radical Ku Klux in Douglas County." (The use of the term "Radical Ku Klux" was a bit of intentional irony, since some of the bands the Alsups had opposed in the years immediately after the Civil War were allied with the Ku Klux Klan.)

Nine days after the *Times* article appeared, Shelt Alsup wrote his own letter to Governor Brown, responding to Hatfield's charges. "Who is John Hatfield?" Alsup asked contemptuously. Answering his rhetorical question, he noted that Hatfield had arrived in Douglas County just one step ahead of the law. Then citing an incident the previous summer in which Hatfield had fired upon some innocent travelers who had camped near Hatfield's spring, Shelt went on to suggest that Hatfield was little more than a ruffian and common outlaw.

William M. Miller, state representative from Douglas County, also rose to the defense of the Alsups. In a letter to Brown dated January 28, 1871 (the same date as Shelt Alsup's letter), Miller described the Alsups as "honorable, law-abiding citizens" and suggested that Hatfield, on the other hand, had "not a very enviable reputation for honesty and veracity."

Hatfield, though, continued to petition the governor. On February 7, 1871, he fired off another letter to Brown describing the outrages perpetrated by the Alsup faction and renewing his request for the governor to send men to Douglas County to restore order. He said that any Democrat, or anyone who dared vote against the Alsups or otherwise oppose them, risked being intimidated, run off, or even killed.

Sometime around the end of March 1871, Hatfield made a trip to Arkansas. Upon his return to Missouri, he stopped at his house in Douglas County on April 4, with plans to continue to Marshfield within a day or two. That evening, about ten men of the Alsup band gathered near his home and kept a menacing eye on him. The next morning, three of the gang fired shots at him as he walked toward his barn.

The following Saturday, from Marshfield, Hatfield wrote

another letter to the governor, describing the incident and also telling Brown about another episode that had happened on or about March 23. A member of the Alsup band named Jeffries was arrested for rape by a local constable, but the lawman allowed the prisoner to go inside his home to change clothes before taking him to jail. Jeffries promptly reappeared with a pistol and told the constable to put down his weapon. When the officer refused, Jeffries shot him dead.

Hatfield told Brown that the Alsups considered anyone who had voted for the governor to be a rebel, and he renewed his call for Brown to send troops to Douglas County to keep order. "Brown's friends have had to suffer by this Alsup band of outlaws," Hatfield complained, "and we 'Brown rebels' respectfully ask of you as law-abiding citizens to compel these outlaws and murderers to be brought to justice before they kill more officers and citizens." Hatfield said that the peaceable citizens of Howell, Texas, Wright, and Ozark counties were talking about forming a vigilante committee to protect themselves from the Alsup gang if Brown did not send help.

Hatfield must have returned to Douglas County shortly after his April 8 letter to Governor Brown, because someone from the Alsup camp calling himself Captain W. Courageous issued an ultimatum to Hatfield in the form of a letter dated April 12, 1871, that was presumably delivered to Hatfield at or near his home. The letter ordered Hatfield to "load your wagon and team and take that rebel that you brout from Arkansaw, take him inside of five dase or your house and barn shall be destroyed by fire." It continued, "I have perval [prevailed?] and saved it til now and all we want is for you to take that nasty Arkansaw rebel out of the state and if you don't you may look out for what comes next. We have good proof that he is a rebel for the melishy liked to beat him to deth last winter, was won year ago and he hast to leave hear in good order and soon, so no more." It was signed, "Captain W. Couragess and Company."

It is obvious from this letter that Hatfield, on his recent trip to Arkansas, had brought someone back whom the Alsups considered a strong rebel sympathizer, but it's not clear who this person was. The identity of the missive's author is also not known, but it was very likely not Shelt Alsup. Shelt's handwriting was more legible and his command of spelling and grammar better than that of Captain Courageous.

Hatfield forwarded the letter to Governor Brown and no doubt renewed his call for protection from the Alsups. But if the governor was swayed by Hatfield's repeated pleas, any state intervention he might have planned in Douglas County came too late to help him. In late May of 1871, a month and a half after he had received the ultimatum, Hatfield was found dead in the road near Fox Creek not far from his home, his body riddled with bullets. A St. Louis newspaper reported that, after initially resisting an Alsup-led "posse" that called at his house, Hatfield had surrendered peacefully and then was shot down in cold blood while being escorted away from his home. The corpse was left lying in the road for some time, the neighbors being unwilling to move it and give it a decent burial for fear of reprisal by the Alsup gang.

The Alsup family continued to control Douglas County politics throughout the early and mid-1870s. Shelt Alsup was elected sheriff and collector in 1874 and reelected in 1876, and other members of the family also served on occasion as county officers.

During that time, Shelt became involved in an incident that would ultimately prove to be his undoing. Details, such as exactly when it took place, remain sketchy, but one story, handed down as oral legend for a number of years before finally being written down in 1938, provides a general outline of the circumstances. An Arkansas man named Doc Cantrell, who was an avid horse racer, happened to be passing through Douglas County, and knowing that the Alsups shared this passion, he challenged them to a race to be held on White River in northern Arkansas at a designated future date. As the appointed time neared, the four Alsup brothers rode

Monument to the Alsup men and their racehorses in northeast Douglas County.

south and found the whole White River territory agog with excitement over the coming contest. A lot of betting took place in Cantrell's village in Baxter County, and both Cantrell and the Alsups placed large bets on their respective horses. The next day, the contestants rode west to Nave's Bend for the race, and Shelt, aboard the Alsup horse, won. Cantrell, alarmed by the outcome, immediately rode home and withdrew the bet he had placed, while the Alsups lingered at Nave's Bend to watch other races. When Shelt learned what Cantrell had done, he rode over to the village, and amid taunts from some of Cantrell's friends about the Alsups being "darn Union Yanks" who cheated at horseracing, he angrily confronted Cantrell. Cantrell finally forked over the money he owed, but the confrontation stirred up old animosities. Fortifying themselves with corn liquor, Cantrell and some of his rebel friends rode out after Alsup, overtook him on the trail, and knocked him unconscious with a club.

When Shelt regained his senses, he found his horse nearby, mounted up, and immediately set out for revenge. He met Cantrell and one of his men at a small tributary of White

River and killed them both in a pistol fight. Although the White River country of northern Arkansas was aroused by the shooting, Alsup made his escape back to Missouri. The Arkansas governor had trouble getting Missouri authorities to serve a warrant for the politically connected sheriff's arrest, particularly since many of Alsup's friends felt he was probably justified in killing the two men.

In the fall election of 1878, however, Hardin H. Vickery defeated Alsup in his bid for a third term as sheriff. Arkansas governor William Miller in late February 1879 sent Missouri governor John S. Phelps a requisition for Alsup's arrest. Phelps issued a warrant on February 28 and gave it to Douglas County state representative Frank Kendall for delivery. (Shelt's brother-in-law, Jesse Cox, was also named in the warrant, but the nature of his involvement in the killing of Cantrell is not known.) Although Vickery was, like Alsup, a former Union soldier, he had run for sheriff on a promise that he would serve every writ that was handed to him, and he meant to keep the promise. The warrant for Alsup's arrest reached Douglas County around March 7, and Vickery promptly set out to serve it.

He had little trouble rounding up a posse of fifteen to twenty men. (Some of the men who volunteered to help serve the warrant doubtlessly nursed grudges against the Alsups because of acts they had committed during their stern control of Douglas County for so many previous years.) Early on Saturday morning, March 8, the posse rode to the Alsup home.

Sheriff Vickery hallooed at the door, and his call was answered by Shelt's wife, Nancy. The sheriff identified himself, told her what he was there for, and advised that her husband should surrender peaceably. Mrs. Alsup said Shelt wasn't home, but Vickery knew better and told her he would batter the door down if her husband didn't come out. He also said she needed to send the children out to get them out of danger. After awhile, several children trooped out, and Mrs. Alsup closed the door behind them.

Several of the posse members then took a fence rail and, using it as a battering ram, broke the door. Nancy Alsup sprang into the doorway with an ax in her hand, defiantly telling the sheriff and his posse to stay out of her house. Shelt Alsup then fired a shot from the interior of the house that struck Vickery in the stomach. He sank to the ground and died almost instantly.

The posse promptly returned fire, and bullets flew fast and furious for several moments. When the posse heard a groan from inside the home, they ceased fire. Nancy Alsup hollered that her husband was dead, and the posse entered the house and found it to be true. To their horror, they also discovered that the Alsups' five-year-old daughter, who had stayed in bed instead of going outside with her siblings, had been killed by a stray shot.

A newspaper at Springfield, the nearest major town, sixty miles away, chronicled the triple killing in a brief story the next week under the matter-of-fact headline "Fatal Affray in Douglas County." It was as though a sheriff and ex-sheriff of the same county killing each other was not particularly out of the ordinary. Considering it was Douglas County, maybe it wasn't.

6

The Daring and Defiant Bob Layton

Robert "Bob" Layton was born about 1858, shortly after his family had arrived in Missouri from Tennessee. The Laytons settled at the mining town of Granby, where Bob grew up as the only boy in a large family of girls. (He had eight sisters.) The father died when Bob was about eight or nine years old, leaving his mother, Malvina, to rear nine kids on her own in the rowdy atmosphere of Granby, where notorious young hellions such as Bud Blount and George Hudson held sway.

Although Layton was several years younger than Bud and George, he was near the same age as some of their younger brothers, and he eventually fell in with the Blount-Hudson gang. About ten o'clock on the night of June 16, 1877, Layton and three other men from Granby rode into the fledgling mining town of Galena, Kansas, about thirty miles away, looking for a man named William "Tiger Bill" St. Clair, against whom at least one of the gang nursed a grudge.

They located their man at Dykeman's restaurant on the town's infamous "Red Hot" Street, where saloons and gambling palaces vied with houses of ill repute for the patronage of the free-spending miners who had flocked to the area in recent weeks. St. Clair and a companion named Harry Campbell were seated at a table in the restaurant taking a late dinner when the quartet of desperadoes strode in. Campbell, who recognized two of the men, hailed the newcomers and started to introduce them to his companion as they approached the table. "Gentlemen, this is my friend Tiger Bill. . . . "

"Yes, we have been looking for Tiger Bill," interrupted one of the men, and the gang pulled out their revolvers and started firing at both Campbell and St. Clair. The first shot struck Campbell in the right shoulder, giving him a flesh wound before he dashed for safety. The next blast hit St. Clair, and he fell mortally wounded.

The gang ran out of the restaurant, mounted up, and galloped out of town. They exchanged shots with several bystanders on the streets of Galena as they rode away, but no one else was injured. Tiger Bill died from his wound about twelve hours later.

It is not known for sure who the other three Granby men with Layton were. It is a good bet, though, that they were members of the Blount-Hudson gang, even if Blount and Hudson themselves may not have been among them. Layton was only nineteen in June of 1877, and he was almost certainly not the leader of the gang who killed Tiger Bill. It is far more likely that either Blount or Hudson was the leader, although Layton was the only one who was identified and whose name was later published in area newspapers in connection with the incident.

What is known for sure about Layton's affiliation with the Blount-Hudson gang around this time is that he and several other men posted bond in Jasper County Court on September 1, 1877, for James Powell, one of the rioters who, along with Hudson and the Blounts, had terrorized Webb City earlier in the year.

And by the time Bob Layton accompanied George Hudson and his brother Jack to Arkansas in early November of 1879, he was a veteran member of the gang. Near dusk on the evening of Friday the seventh, the trio, driving two covered wagons, passed hurriedly through Batesville along the main streets, and they crossed a bayou on the edge of town without pausing to let their teams drink. They camped just outside town, though, and came back into Batesville later that night.

After trying unsuccessfully at one store to buy corn to feed their animals, they went to another store, operated by E. W. Clapp, and inquired about obtaining a wagon and team to haul goods to nearby Newport. Clapp told them to come back in the morning and, because they were strangers, they would have to be identified by someone in Batesville. They assured the storekeeper that they could give references, and George Hudson, in an apparent attempt to gain the man's confidence, asked him whether he had any of the good peach brandy like he used to keep. When Clapp said he did, Hudson turned to Layton and remarked, "Let's take a drink. He keeps good brandy."

"No," Layton said, "whiskey is good enough for me. I'll just take some bourbon."

After George Hudson and Bob Layton sampled Clapp's liquor supply, the three men left, saying they would return the next morning. They started making the rounds of the town's saloons: first the Pearl Saloon and then Holmes's Saloon, located in the Southern Hotel. At the latter establishment, Hudson started arguing with a man named S. L. Gwinn concerning an accusation that Hudson's pals the Blount brothers had stolen some horses from a local farmer named Dennison three years earlier (a charge that was very likely true). Hudson claimed to have heard about the allegation two years earlier at Hot Springs, and he presumably wanted to know who was doing the accusing.

Meanwhile, Layton, giving his name as Davis, struck up a conversation at the bar with a man named Weast. When both Layton and George Hudson started to get boisterous, Jack Hudson, who had not been drinking, tried to calm them down, warning them not to "get drunk and raise hell again." But Jack's admonitions were to no avail.

When an acquaintance of Weast named Joe Price entered the saloon, Weast called for him to come over so he could introduce him to his new "pard." Weast started to present Layton as "Mr. Davis," but the drunken Layton told the two men they were both loafers and he didn't want to have anything to do with them.

Price retorted, "You ought not to say that," and Layton responded by punching him on the side of the face. When Weast came to Price's defense, Hudson struck Weast in the face in the same manner. Price then went for a billiard cue, and both Hudson and Layton drew their pistols. Hudson fired an errant shot at Price as he and his sidekick crashed through the glass in the front door to make their escape.

On their way back to camp, Hudson and Layton overtook a young man named Dick Reid who was headed home along the same road. They demanded to know his name, kicked and slapped him a time or two, and stole his hat. When he remonstrated, one of the pair struck him a blow to the head with a pistol. Hudson and Layton then continued to their camp, where Hudson armed himself with a Henry rifle, and the desperate duo waited in ambush to see whether they might be followed.

Reid, meanwhile, went back into town to report what had happened, and a posse immediately formed and gave chase. They discovered the pair among a thicket of cedar trees and demanded their surrender. The desperadoes answered with a volley of shots, and the posse returned fire, killing one of the outlaws' horses. Continuing to press their advantage, the deputies got so near in the darkness that the engagement turned into hand-to-hand fighting. Layton fled from the close-quarters combat, but Hudson stood his ground and knocked one of the posse down with a pistol blow. A second lawman, though, knocked the villain down in the same manner, and several others jumped in to subdue the violent Hudson.

A LITTLE WAR.

Burnt Powder Smelt by Some of Our Boys.

A VISIT FROM NEVER-TO-BE-TAKEN BOYS.

One Man Captured—Another Shot Dead in His Tracks.

Blood to be Seen Even Now Upon Our Streets.

EXCITEMENT FOR A TIME HIGH.

Violations of the Law Wiped Out With Blood.

OUR TOWN WIDE-AWAKE AND ON THE ALERT.

Clipping from a Batesville newspaper describing Layton and Hudson's raid on the town.

Layton's and the Hudsons' animals and wagons were confiscated, and George was taken back to Batesville and locked in the county jail. He was arraigned the next morning (Saturday) and the case set for later that day, but it was continued until Monday. Shortly after dark on Saturday night, the "daring and defiant" Layton, as a Batesville newspaper called him, ventured back into town to try to break Hudson out of jail. (Jack Hudson, meanwhile, had hightailed it back to Granby to avoid being dragged into any more trouble by his reckless brother and the equally rash Bob Layton.)

Citizens of Batesville had been watching throughout the day for any attempt to free Hudson, and one of them spotted Layton as he approached the downtown area. Hailing a nearby police officer, the citizen pointed him out as one of the men involved in the affray at the Southern Hotel the previous night. The police officer overtook Layton and demanded to know his name. Layton replied, "Lane." As the two men continued together down Main Street, the lawman told "Lane" that he had a writ for Layton's arrest and proposed to escort him to Holmes's Saloon so that he could be positively identified one way or the other. Layton told the officer he was not going with him and turned down Spring Street. The policeman yelled for the fugitive to halt, but when Layton reached for his pistol instead, the officer fired a single shot that struck the fleeing suspect in the back of the head and passed through his brain, killing him almost instantly.

A coroner's inquest into the killing was held the next day. One man testified before the jury that he had known Layton for several years and that "his character was that of a desperado and gambler." The coroner's jury concluded that "Robert Layton came to his death by a pistol shot, fired by an officer of the law, in the faithful performance of his official duty, and that said officer was justifiable in so doing." After the inquest, Layton's body was "decently interred" at Batesville's Oakland Cemetery. Thus was cut short the promising criminal career of twenty-two-year-old Bob Layton, while his sidekick George Hudson gave bond a week or so later and absconded to Colorado, where he promptly resumed his one-man campaign to rewrite the criminal record book.

7

Britton the Bold

Sixty-five-year-old George Britton and his sixty-year-old wife, Catherine, were two of the people the editor of the *Neosho Times* had in mind when he lamented in 1875 that many parents in the Missouri community permitted their sons "to roam the streets at will, day and night, from the time they can walk." He added, "The education they receive in such a school eminently qualifies them for the gibbet or the penitentiary." The criminal record of the Brittons' son Lane from 1875 forward leaves little doubt that he indeed qualified for the scaffold or prison, but he must have learned something else on the streets of Neosho, too, because he somehow managed to escape both.

Young Britton graduated from the school of idle time into the real world of crime near Christmas of 1875, when he was just seventeen years old. On the night of December 23, he was whiling away the evening at a "house of ill-fame . . . kept by an abandoned strumpet named Lizzie Sanford" in Neosho when Wiley Huffaker and two other drunken young men called at the door and asked admission. (The *Times* editor claimed Huffaker came from one of the most respectable families in McDonald County but failed to explain why such an upstanding citizen was calling at such an establishment.) Britton and Lizzie refused entrance to the three men, but Lizzie referred them to another house on a nearby corner. After getting no answer there, the three decided that Huffaker should go back to Lizzie's establishment alone.

Huffaker returned and rapped loudly on the door, but Lizzie once again told him to leave and warned him that if he didn't he would be shot. "Shoot and be damned," Huffaker retorted, and Britton promptly accepted the challenge, firing a shot through the door that struck Huffaker in the head and killed him almost instantly.

Britton hurried to his parents' home, where his father supplied him with a horse and his mother gave him money, and he then "left for parts unknown." The next day, a coroner's jury found that Huffaker had come to his death at the hands of Lane Britton and that Lizzie Sanford was an accessory before and after the fact. Warrants for the arrests of both parties were issued, and a $100 reward was offered for Britton's capture. Lizzie was arrested that day and taken before a judge. Her case was scheduled to be heard on Christmas Day, but she was discharged when the prosecution failed to appear. (Lizzie later moved to Joplin and was tried and convicted in Jasper County in 1877, under the name Lizzie Bobbett, of luring a young girl into a bawdy house.)

Meanwhile, Britton came back to Neosho a day or two after his crime and turned himself in. He had a preliminary hearing on December 28 and was committed to jail to await the action of a grand jury. He was later indicted for murder, but his trial in the fall of 1876 ended in a hung jury. The case was then moved to Greene County for a change of venue, and Britton gave bond and went free while awaiting retrial. The case was finally heard in Springfield in the spring of 1878. The defense claimed that both Britton and Lizzie Sanford were in fear for their lives when Huffaker rapped on the door and demanded entrance to Lizzie's house, and Britton was acquitted on the grounds of justifiable homicide.

Returning to Newton County, Lane Britton got into a row at Granby with a miner named Bishop on or about August 1, 1879. Apparently, Britton allowed Bishop to use his team and wagon, but when he demanded payment, Bishop refused. The pair argued, and Britton ended up striking Bishop several times. On the morning of the second, deputy city marshal Jack Hudson undertook to arrest Britton on a charge of assault. Hudson's father was the Granby city marshal and several of his sons had served as deputies at one time or another, but all the male members of the family were considered ruffians. Jack's brother George had killed two or three men and would later kill at least three more (see chapter 4). Jack himself had been involved in two or three shooting scrapes. So, it is not terribly surprising that Britton fled when he saw Hudson approaching. The deputy marshal fired several times at the suspect, hitting him at least once in the leg, but Britton made his escape.

About the time of this incident, Britton moved to Empire City, Kansas (present-day Galena), where, at the time of the 1880 census, he was living in the boardinghouse of M. A. Lane and working as a blacksmith. Shortly afterward, he married nineteen-year-old Mary Ellen Rawles.

Around the first of the year of 1883, the couple moved across the state line to the new mining camp of Blende City, Missouri, about eight miles northwest of Joplin at the southwestern edge of Carl Junction, where Britton engaged in lead mining. He was named city marshal of the fledgling town in the spring of 1883, but according to a Joplin newspaper, instead of being a peacemaker, he became a "terror to the place." Shortly after being appointed the chief law officer of Blende, he grew incensed with the mayor, ripped his marshal's star from his coat, and trampled it underfoot. Then he reportedly mounted his horse and rode up and down the street with his revolver drawn, as a demonstration that he meant to "run the town." He was subsequently arrested and fined for his outburst.

After the incident at Granby in the summer of 1879, Bishop had declined to swear out a warrant against Britton, and, according to Britton's own later version of the story, the two men had settled their dispute to the satisfaction of each. However, Jack Hudson, who now served as a Newton County deputy sheriff, apparently still nursed a grudge over Britton's resisting arrest, and in the summer of 1883, he managed to convince Bishop to swear out a warrant against Britton. The trouble Britton had caused at Blende had likely alerted Hudson to his whereabouts.

At any rate, Hudson and Granby constable Aaron Davis came to Jasper County on June 28, 1883, with a warrant for Britton's arrest on a charge of felonious assault, and Constable G. G. "Gid" Davis of East Joplin joined the posse. The three men started toward Blende, but before they reached Britton's home, the two Davises found him at Carl Junction unloading mineral from his wagon. Britton balked at the idea of going back to Granby with Aaron Davis and asked instead to be taken to the Newton County seat at Neosho. But he offered no serious resistance (at least according to what he later told his brother Silas) until he learned that Jack Hudson was a member of the posse. Becoming alarmed when Hudson showed up and plotting an escape, he asked permission to take his team and wagon home before going with the lawmen. The request was granted. The two constables accompanied Britton to Blende, while Deputy Hudson went to ready a team to take the prisoner to Newton County.

At his Blende home, Britton put his horses in the stable and asked permission to go inside the house and get some clothes. The two lawmen stood a few steps outside the door as Britton entered the home. Moments later, he sprang from the house and pointed a revolver at Aaron Davis. "Drop your pistol, you son of a bitch!" the outlaw swore.

When Aaron Davis obliged, Britton struck him across the face with the revolver, knocking him to the ground. Gid Davis, taking cover behind a corner of the house, fired a shot at the desperado with a small pistol, but it missed. Britton returned fire, striking Gid in the head, and the Joplin constable fell mortally wounded. Britton then turned back to Aaron Davis, still lying prostrate on the ground, and shot him through the head, killing him instantly. (In Britton's own version of the story, he shot the two constables only after they each fired at him first.)

Britton inspected his bloody work a moment, then went to the stable and brought out his horses. Mounting one and leaving the other loose to follow, he rode to the front door of his house, where his wife handed him another pistol and a cartridge belt. He strapped the belt to his waist and bid his wife goodbye. With the pistol in one hand and the bridle reins in the other, he rode off in a southwesterly direction, trailed by the loose horse.

Help soon arrived at the scene of the shooting. Aaron Davis's body was removed for burial, while the gravely wounded Gid Davis was taken back to Joplin, where he died several hours later. That evening, Deputy Hudson went back to Newton County empty handed.

After authorities had left, "Britton the Bold," as one newspaperman called the killer, came back home to see his wife. He tarried several days in the Blende area, where it was reported that he "makes no attempt at seclusion but walks around with the air of a conqueror." One man who talked to Britton reported that the fugitive cited his fear of Hudson as the cause of his desperate action. He claimed Hudson was just trying to get him out on the road and then would have found some pretext to shoot him, which was not an unreasonable apprehension, given Hudson's bent toward gunplay.

The Jasper County court offered a reward of $100 for Britton's arrest on July 2, and the fugitive started lying low, although he apparently remained in the general area for at least another week. On Tuesday, July 10, the editor of the *Joplin Daily Herald* reported facetiously in the newspaper's "personal" or society column, "Mr. Lane Britton, late mayor of Blende, was visiting friends near Neosho Sunday. Mr. Britton of late is somewhat retired in his habits, confining his society to a secret circle of intimate friends." The *Herald* reported on July 11 that Britton's wife had left Blende and on July 12 that she had sold a team and wagon in nearby Webb City, presumably in preparation for joining her fugitive husband in his flight.

By the time a warrant for Britton's arrest for the murder of Aaron Davis was issued in Jasper County on July 22, the couple had apparently already left for parts unknown, as no trace of Britton or his wife was reported for the next two years. In March of 1885, Missouri governor John S. Marmaduke signed a proclamation offering a $250 reward for Britton's capture, and descriptions of the fugitive were sent out to law-enforcement agencies across the country.

Meanwhile, Britton and his wife had made their way to Tom Green County, Texas, where Britton lived briefly

Lane Britton and his wife, circa 1885. (Courtesy Linda Childers and Judy Sire)

under the name of Tom Beard. They then moved on to New Mexico Territory, where they joined Silas Britton. (Another of Lane's brothers, Wiley, later gained fame as the author of several books about the Civil War.) About the middle of 1884, Britton, his wife, and his brother moved to Globe in Arizona Territory, where Britton found work as a teamster. The couple and their new baby, again accompanied by Silas, moved to Phoenix in mid- to late June of 1885 and took up residence in a house located just a block from the Maricopa County courthouse. Britton introduced himself around town as James Britton and started working as a blacksmith, the same occupation he had been engaged in at the time of the 1880 census.

About the time Britton and his family moved to Phoenix, Deputy W. T. Rice of Neosho was dispatched to Tom Green County, Texas, to bring back a fugitive named Pomp Chester. He learned from Chester that Britton had lived briefly in Tom Green County and had since moved on to Arizona Territory. Rice passed this intelligence on to Arizona authorities, along with a description of the fugitive. After some investigation, Maricopa County officers arrested Britton on August 14 as a possible fugitive from justice and then wired Missouri officials informing them of the arrest and requesting extradition papers. The prisoner was described as standing about five feet five inches tall and weighing about 165 pounds, with blue eyes, a light complexion, and light-colored mustache. He was said to have a receding forehead, a scar on the center of his head, and the marks of a gunshot wound on his right knee (presumably inflicted by Jack Hudson).

Britton retained a lawyer and was discharged on a writ of habeas corpus on August 17, but he was immediately rearrested on a warrant from another judge. Brought before the court, the fugitive admitted that he knew Lane Britton, Lane was in fact his cousin, and he had even furnished his kinsman with money to make his escape, but he claimed that he himself was not Lane Britton. The judge, though, ruled that there was enough evidence to hold the defendant on examination for twenty days. A photo of the prisoner was taken and forwarded to Missouri for identification purposes.

The next day, August 18, Britton's lawyer filed another writ of habeas corpus, and the fugitive was brought before the county court commissioner from his jail cell about four o'clock in the afternoon. An hour or two later, the case had still not been decided, and it was continued until ten o'clock the next day.

As Britton was being escorted from the courtroom back downstairs to the jail late in the afternoon, he was met at the foot of the steps by his wife, who had the couple's baby in her arms. She handed the infant to Britton, and he asked to speak to his wife a moment in the jailer's room before going to his cell. The request was granted, and the jailer, a man named Belyea, retired to the adjoining sheriff's office, where he laid aside his pistol. A deputy on duty left to go to dinner, and Belyea went back into the room where Britton was talking to his wife. Britton's attorney, A. C. Baker, also showed up and spoke with his client awhile. After the lawyer left, Belyea announced that it was time for Britton to go back to his cell. As the jailer was unlocking the big iron door, Britton suddenly whipped out a pistol (apparently slipped to him by his wife), pointed it at Belyea's head, and told the jailer "to stand still and not utter a word or he would blow his brains out."

Britton bounded out of the courthouse and dashed across the courthouse square and a vacant lot to his nearby home, where a horse that was already saddled and bridled awaited him. Mounting the horse, which was also carrying a saddlebag of provisions and had a Winchester rifle strapped to its back, Britton galloped away. "So quickly was the plan carried out," according to a Phoenix newspaper, "that Britton was riding rapidly away before anyone could realize the fact."

At a ranch four and a half miles northwest of Phoenix, Britton abandoned his exhausted horse, having covered the distance in an estimated fifteen minutes. The fugitive compelled the rancher, a Mr. Prisbrey, to supply him with another mount and, after rapidly changing the saddle, was again "off with the wind." Later the same night, Britton, at the point of a gun, also forced a second man, whom he met along the road, to trade horses with him.

Maricopa County undersheriff Frank P. Trott led a posse in pursuit of Britton, and the lawmen were about ten minutes behind him when they reached Prisbrey's ranch. Around midnight, though, they stopped to rest for the night when it was determined that Britton was "off the road and was traveling about in a confused manner." The posse resumed the chase early the next morning but lost track of the fugitive a day or two later.

On August 18, the day Britton escaped, Albert Morehouse, Missouri's acting governor, finally got around to issuing the requisition for the fugitive's extradition, but by then it was too late. Morehouse placed the requisition in the hands of Deputy Rice of Newton County, who had been commissioned to go after the prisoner, and Rice promptly set out to bring him back. Before he had gone far, though, Rice was intercepted with the news that Britton had escaped. Returning to Newton County, he nevertheless forwarded the requisition by mail on August 20 to the governor of Arizona, in case Britton was recaptured. The governor sent it on to the Maricopa County sheriff's office. Undersheriff Trott replied to the governor, explaining that Britton had escaped and had not been recaptured. He complained that if extradition papers had been issued in a more timely fashion, his office would have had more authority for holding the fugitive. Therefore, he would not have been released on a habeas corpus writ, "affording the opportunity for Britton to perfect his plan, aided by his attorney, and make his bold and successful dash for liberty."

Trott told the governor that, since Britton had escaped, his office did not need the warrant. However, he added that

Britton was last seen in Yavapai County north of Maricopa
and that the sheriff there might call upon the governor for
the requisition if the fugitive was recaptured.

No such luck! Apparently Britton had learned something
about lying low and avoiding capture when he was on the
run the first time. Governor Stone of Missouri issued a
proclamation on December 20, 1895, similar to the one
Governor Marmaduke had issued over ten years earlier,
offering a $250 reward for the fugitive's capture. But by
that time, "Bloody Britton" had long since vanished. In
1906, a man thought to be Britton was arrested at Durant
in Oklahoma Territory, but the prisoner proved not to be
him. The real Britton was never officially heard from again,
although information from a family descendant suggests
that he lived out his days under an assumed name and died
around 1920 near Hollywood, California.

8

Pink Fagg: A Notorious Gambler and Desperate Character

When Joel Pinkney Fagg was growing up in Springfield, Missouri, during the Civil War era, his father was a storekeeper who supplemented the income from his grocery business with revenue from a variety of banned activities. James H. Fagg, catering to the many soldiers in the military-headquarters town, repeatedly ran afoul of the law for selling liquor without a license, maintaining a gambling operation, and similar offenses. As a young man in Springfield, J. P. Fagg, or "Pink" as he was usually called, was exposed to the underworld of gambling and alcohol, a world that would ultimately prove to be his downfall.

Pink Fagg's name first appears in court records in connection with a civil suit he filed in Greene County in early November of 1873. The twenty-two-year-old Fagg claimed that another man had possession of a Texas saddle that belonged to him. The case was dismissed later in the month when the saddle was returned without court action.

Less than two years later, though, Fagg got himself into serious trouble when he tried to steal a large sum of money from a Springfield resident. On June 20, 1875, Fagg threw a container of chloroform into a room where sixty-five-year-old Jacob Painter was sleeping, adjacent to his gun shop on Olive Street, with the idea of inducing such a deep slumber that the thief would be able to slip in and steal $2,700 in cash that Painter had on the premises. The plan failed, though, and charges of attempted grand larceny were brought against Fagg. He was indicted at the November term of Greene County Circuit Court and lodged in the county jail to await trial, but Fagg petitioned the court for a change of venue, suggesting that the citizens of Greene County were so prejudiced against him that he couldn't get a fair hearing there. Several of Fagg's acquaintances filed an affidavit in support of the request, testifying that they had heard many citizens of the county "express themselves adversely to said J. P. Fagg—that they well knew that said Fagg was guilty—that he had been stealing for a long time in Springfield and Greene County but was not caught," and that he should have been sent to the penitentiary some time ago.

Fagg was granted a change of venue to Christian County in March of 1876, and he was transferred to the county jail at Ozark. At the April term of the Christian County Circuit Court, he was convicted of attempted grand larceny and sentenced to two years in the state penitentiary. Upon his arrival at Jefferson City on April 26, he was described as five feet ten and a half inches tall with auburn hair, blue eyes, and a fair complexion, and his occupation was listed as cigar maker.

Fagg was released on October 18, 1877, under the three-fourths rule, and he joined a younger brother, Bud, in the booming lead-mining town of Joplin, seventy miles west of Springfield. With its assortment of gamblers, prostitutes, and other ne'er-do-wells, it was exactly the kind of place the Faggs were used to, having grown up in the tumultuous Civil War climate of Springfield. They soon started engaging in the same types of activities that their father had carried on back home.

During the late seventies, Bud Fagg was charged in Jasper County Court with several offenses involving gambling and liquor sales, and in mid-December of 1879 Pink Fagg was charged with betting on a faro bank. The case came to trial almost a year later, and he was convicted and paid a fine and court costs of about twenty dollars.

In the meantime, Fagg, who reportedly was liberal with his money and made friends easily, had met and married a seventeen-year-old girl named Elizabeth Tweedy on September 19, 1880. According to a later report, he had taken the girl out of "a house of ill-fame" and told her that, if he ever caught her in such a house again, he would kill her. The fact that Elizabeth Tweedy was listed in her father's household at the time of the 1880 census calls this assertion into question. But at any rate, by September of 1881, only a year after she and Pink had married, Lizzie Fagg had abandoned her husband and was living in Carthage at a bawdy house run by a woman named Mollie Moore.

Upon learning Lizzie's whereabouts on September 14, Pink Fagg flew into a rage and announced to his friends in Joplin that he was going to Carthage to kill his wife, but they passed the threat off as mere bluster. Pink, however, set out, in the company of a man named Panley Cooley, to carry out the boast, and the two men called that night at Mollie Moore's house in Carthage. Mollie met them at the door and told them Lizzie was not there, but Fagg and his companion walked inside anyway, with Cooley going to the rear of the house. Fagg, who had already earned a reputation as a "notorious gambler" and "desperate character," pulled out a revolver and ordered Mollie to light a lantern and show him to all the rooms. He searched the rooms without finding his wife, but as he prepared to leave, Lizzie walked through the back door. As she started toward the stairway, he pointed his revolver at her and fired. Lizzie fell with a wound to the head.

After the shooting, Fagg ran out of the house toward the railroad, while Mollie rushed to the square to sound the alarm. Carthage police made a futile search for Fagg, and two doctors promptly went to Mollie's house to attend to the injured woman. They found that a .44 caliber ball had entered the left side of her face near the base of her nose and exited below her right ear. After treating the wound, the doctors expressed the opinion that it would prove fatal.

CAPIAS—WARRANT FROM CIRCUIT COURT FOR ANY INDICTMENT.

(Wagner's Statutes, page 10...)

STATE OF MISSOURI. } ss.
COUNTY OF JASPER.

The State of Missouri to the Sheriff of *Jasper* County—GREETING:

WE COMMAND YOU TO TAKE *Pink Fagg*

if he be found in your County, and him safely keep, so that you have his body before the Judge of our Circuit Court, at the Court House in Carthage, within and for the said County of Jasper, on the .... Monday in *Instanter* next, then and there, before our said Judge, to answer an indictment preferred against him by the Grand Jurors of the State of Missouri, empannelled, sworn and charged to enquire in and for the body of the County of *Jasper* aforesaid, for

Assault with intent to Kill

whereof he stands indicted. And this you shall in no wise omit. And have you then and there this writ.

WITNESS my hand as Clerk, and the seal of our said Court hereto affixed. Done at office in Carthage, in the County aforesaid, on this *23* day of *Sept* A. D. 188*1*

W. A. Williams CLERK.

Jasper County warrant indicting Pink Fagg for felonious assault on his wife. (Courtesy Jasper County Records Center)

Despite the doctors' dire prediction, Lizzie not only survived but made virtually a full recovery. Her fugitive husband, meanwhile, was featured in the *National Police Gazette*. While on the run from the law, he made his way to Florida, where he reportedly rusticated "among the orange groves" for awhile before returning to Missouri and giving himself up in Joplin on November 14. He was charged with felonious assault, but the case was dismissed in March of 1882 when the witnesses against him, including Lizzie Fagg and Mollie Moore, could not be located.

Fagg got into another difficulty in 1885 at a Fourth of July celebration in Pierce City. He and Ed Whilam, a bartender at the Decatur House Saloon, were among a group "sporting with fireworks" in front of the saloon when someone knocked a lit Roman candle out of Fagg's hand. A small boy picked it up and it went off, striking Fagg in the back and burning a hole in his shirt. Fagg followed Whilam into the saloon and asked who had knocked the Roman candle out of his hand. He was told at first that no one in the saloon was responsible for the deed, but as he started to leave, Whilam said in a joking manner that he had done it. Fagg whirled around and threw the stub of a cigar at the barkeeper. Whilam ducked behind the counter and, according to some witnesses, grabbed a glass or bottle. Fagg marched toward the bar, drew his pistol, extended it across the counter, and fired randomly at his crouching target. The bullet passed through Whilam's left leg and lodged in his right calf.

Fagg made his escape but was soon captured and charged with assault with intent to kill. The case was tried during the August 1885 term of the Lawrence County Circuit Court, and he was convicted and sentenced to two years in the state penitentiary. When he was received at the prison on September 12, he was described in similar terms as those used when he arrived at the facility in 1876, except he was now sporting a mustache and was noted to have a prominent nose, and his occupation had evolved from cigar maker to "tobacconist." He gave no religious preference. His ability to read and write was noted, and he was listed as "intemperate," or given to hard drinking. As was the case during his previous imprisonment, he was released early after serving three-fourths of his term. He was discharged on March 2, 1887.

Fagg's second stay in Jefferson City apparently did even less to rehabilitate him than his first, since it took him less time to get in trouble again. Upon his release, he drifted to Fort Smith, Arkansas, and also was a transient visitor to Texas and Leadville, Colorado, hitting the saloons and gambling houses along the way. Fagg was "holding forth professionally" at the LeGrande Saloon in Fort Smith on Saturday night, July 16, 1887, when former Confederate major Alexander S. Doran came into the establishment under the influence of liquor. Doran, a notorious gambler and reputed killer of nine men, had been involved a couple of years earlier in a violent feud with Frank Flynn over control of Hot Springs. A prior bad feeling existed between Fagg and Doran, "the bone of contention being a girl of easy virtue known as Dot Rowland," who had "for some time been the mistress of Doran." The two men renewed their disagreement at the saloon, arguing periodically all night long. Finally, around midnight, a police officer separated them, suggesting that they go home. They ambled out of the saloon as though to obey the order, with the unarmed Fagg trailing Doran.

Accompanied by "Big Mike" McCulloch, Doran started dilatorily toward home, crossing Garrison Street and pausing a few steps beyond the door of the Phoenix Saloon. Meanwhile, Charlie Christian, an acquaintance of Fagg from their days together in the Missouri State Penitentiary, slipped Fagg a .44 caliber Smith and Wesson five-shot revolver, and Fagg stalked across the street and opened fire. His second shot dropped Doran, but the major managed to draw his .44 Colt as he fell. From a sitting position, he "fired three times, but shot very wild, evidently being dazed or too much under the influence of liquor to use his gun with that degree of marksmanship shown by him in similar contests heretofore." As Doran's gun was blazing, Fagg answered with the remaining three shots from his pistol and then darted around the corner of a building.

Only one blast from Fagg's final barrage found its mark, but that was enough. The gravely wounded Doran was taken to a room at the LaGrande Hotel for treatment and then moved the next day to Dot Rowland's home, where he died on July 19, three days after the shooting. He was buried the following day in the Fort Smith city cemetery.

Fagg turned himself in to a deputy sheriff after the shooting and was taken to jail. Christian and McCulloch were held as accomplices in the crime but later released. Pete and Bud Fagg arrived in Fort Smith a couple of days after the shooting and employed a team of lawyers for their brother's defense. Fagg's preliminary hearing in Sebastian County Court in Fort Smith concluded on July 26, and he was bound over for trial on a charge of first-degree murder.

With a change of venue to the Greenwood District of Sebastian County, Fagg's trial began in early January of 1888. The prosecution witnesses stated that Doran did not draw his pistol until after he had already been shot, but those testifying for the defense claimed that he drew first, and other conflicting evidence was presented. In addition, the defense called several witnesses, including famous detective W. A. Pinkerton, who testified to the notorious character of the victim. On January 7, the jury convicted Fagg on a lesser charge of manslaughter and sentenced him to three and half years in the state penitentiary.

The light sentence didn't sit well with law-enforcement officers in Fort Smith. On the weekend after the verdict was announced, they rounded up Mike McCulloch, Charlie Christian, and Jack Fagg (another brother of Pink), who had "been loafing around" town, and arrested them on vagrancy charges. Bud Fagg, though, showed up the next day to bail them out, and the following week they were acquitted of the charges. (A fourth brother of Pink Fagg, Alonzo, had been assaulted and killed on the streets of Springfield in 1879.)

Despite Fagg's lenient sentence, the verdict was immediately appealed to the Arkansas Supreme Court, which, in a ruling issued in June of 1888, affirmed the jury's finding. Fagg was transferred on June 22 from the county jail in Fort Smith to the state prison in Little Rock to begin his sentence.

After his release around 1891, Fagg married; moved to Dennison, Texas, where his old pal Charlie Christian lived; and apparently managed to stay out of serious trouble the rest of his life. He was residing in Tulsa, Oklahoma, in 1910 and was engaged in selling liquor. His widow, Nettie, was still living there ten years later, the notorious Pink Fagg having died in the meantime.

9

The Hudspeth-Watkins Case:
A Criminal Intimacy

On December 9, 1886, forty-one-year-old George Watkins and fifty-year-old Andrew "Andy" J. Hudspeth, whose families lived together in Blythe Township of Marion County, Arkansas, drove in Watkins's wagon to the county seat of Yellville, eight miles to the east, to sell a bale of cotton. It was nearing dark by the time the transaction was completed and the pair started back toward home. George Watkins never got there.

When Hudspeth arrived home alone with Watkins's wagon and team, he told Rebecca Watkins that her husband might come back and he might never come back. He explained to the woman and her eleven-year-old son that Watkins had come partway home before giving up the wagon and team and striking out alone to go work on the railroad.

Mrs. Watkins, though, knew better. She and her husband had moved from Benton County to Marion County, where she had relatives, around 1880. But she had gotten to know Andy Hudspeth only the previous spring when he had come to work on her husband's farm, bringing his family with him. Both families shared the same house, and the intimate arrangements proved too tempting for Hudspeth and his partner's wife. Described by one newspaper report as "very prepossessing" and endowed with "a fine figure," the thirty-eight-year-old Mrs. Watkins entered with Hudspeth into what one observer called "unholy relations" and another dubbed "a criminal intimacy" around "fodder pulling time" (late summer or early fall) of 1886. The two lovers soon began to plot how they could be together, but Rebecca worried that she might lose her son, Isaiah, if she and Andy simply ran away together. Apparently willing to share his lover with her lawfully wedded husband, Hudspeth suggested that he might leave his wife and kids and move away with the Watkins family. George, though, would not hear of such a proposition.

"Damn him and let him go to hell," Hudspeth declared upon learning of Watkins's rejection of the idea. He told Rebecca not to have anything more to do with her husband, and the lovestruck pair began to entertain desperate measures.

Meeting secretly with Hudspeth in the kitchen of the common home a few nights before the trip to Yellville, Rebecca declared her love for him. She suggested that, if it were not for George, she could keep her son and have all of George's property, too. But with George around, if Isaiah ever got mad at Andy, the boy would go to his father and she would never see him again. When Hudspeth suggested that he might be able to do something, Mrs. Watkins merely cautioned him that, if he was going to "do anything," he shouldn't do it near home. Neither Andy nor Rebecca explicitly mentioned murder, but both parties understood the meaning of their conversation.

Now, the diabolical plot had apparently been carried out. Late on the evening of December 9, after returning alone from Yellville, Hudspeth came to Rebecca's bed. He whispered that he was leaving the house for awhile and that, if any of his family missed him, she was to say that he had gone to see about some stock in the field. Hudspeth was gone for about an hour and a half or two hours. Rebecca didn't know where he went, but a couple of days later, when she asked him whether he "had everything hid so it would never be found," he said he did.

On the morning of the tenth, Rebecca inspected her husband's wagon and noticed a lot of blood on the bed and the right front wheel. She noticed, too, that the hatchet George always kept in the wagon was missing. She also saw George's overcoat with blood on it. She told Hudspeth that was "a bad job bringing that coat home" and that he should have left it with George. A few days later, Andy took the coat several miles south to the Greasy Creek area where he used to live and, according to what he later told Rebecca, sold it to a mover. Back home, he gave Rebecca thirty-five dollars, which he said he had taken from the coat.

Isaiah also saw the wagon on the morning of the tenth, and when he noticed the blood, he assumed it was his father's and started crying. Hudspeth assured him that the blood got there from some pigs that he and George had hauled for a man a couple of miles west of Yellville.

A few days after the trip to Yellville, a neighbor named William T. Dobbs came to the Watkins-Hudspeth home and inquired of Rebecca where her husband was. She hesitated at first but finally said that he had gone to Harrison to work on the railroad. Dobbs asked why George hadn't taken his team with him, but Mrs. Watkins made no answer. At this point, Hudspeth came into the house and, in reply to similar inquiries from Dobbs, merely repeated that Watkins had gone to work on the railroad.

A week or two after George's disappearance, Rebecca asked Hudspeth whether she had better not go to her father's house in Boone County to keep down suspicion. He agreed, and Rebecca and Isaiah went to stay with her father, Henry Barkhimer, who lived near Harrison. Hudspeth visited her there a few days later when she was getting ready to leave for Fayetteville, where, she told her father, she was going to join her husband. After she started on the journey, Hudspeth overtook her on the road and spent the night in the wagon with her and Isaiah, all three of them sleeping under the same cover. Upon reaching Fayetteville, Rebecca wrote to her father that George had been killed working on the railroad.

When the circumstances surrounding George Watkins's

disappearance finally came to public light on February 1, 1887, foul play was immediately suspected. Why would George Watkins have abandoned his wagon and team in the middle of the night within a few miles of his home and started on foot to go work on the railroad without even taking his gloves with him? Deputy Sheriff George Lawson arrested Hudspeth on suspicion and lodged him in the county jail at Yellville, pending further investigation.

A search for Watkins's body turned up no evidence, but Deputy Lawson meant to get to the bottom of this mystery. On February 3, he went to Fayetteville to track down Rebecca Watkins and brought her back to Yellville on February 8. Called to testify the next day at the preliminary examination of Andy Hudspeth, she freely admitted her romantic involvement with the defendant and her role in plotting to get rid of her husband. She described the circumstances of her husband's disappearance, including the bloody wagon and the missing hatchet, which she implied might have been the murder weapon. She said she was sure the missing man had been killed by the defendant. Meanwhile, Hudspeth, according to the *Yellville Mountain Echo*, remained "as dumb as an oyster on the subject."

Isaiah Watkins also took the stand at the hearing and corroborated his mother's testimony pertaining to the blood on the wagon, the missing hatchet, and Andy Hudspeth's spending the night with him and his mother on the road to Fayetteville.

After the hearing, Justice of the Peace A. J. Noe ordered the prisoner to be held for murder in the first degree, and Rebecca Watkins was bound over to appear as a witness. Failing to give bond, she was placed in the custody of Deputy Lawson at his residence, and Hudspeth was taken back to jail. The search for Watkins's body continued but without success.

Late on the night of July 10, 1887, a mob of men wearing long black coats and masks rode up to the residence of Deputy

Lawson, barged into his house, disarmed him, and kidnapped Rebecca Watkins. Screaming in terror and pleading for her life, she was taken to a nearby stand of cedar trees, where a rope was placed around her neck in an attempt to scare her into making further confessions about the murder of her husband, but she wailed that she had already told everything she knew at the hearing. She said Hudspeth was supposed to kill Watkins and did kill him but she didn't know where the body was. Deputy Lawson arrived under guard and told the mob not to hang her, but they threatened to hang him, too. Instead, they marched both captives back to the deputy's house before releasing them and then galloped out of town, punctuating their flight with gunfire.

Later in July, shortly before Hudspeth was scheduled to go to trial, a fire destroyed the indictment against him, and a second indictment by a new grand jury had to be brought and drawn up. The trial was set for the August term of the Marion County Circuit Court, and George Watkins's relatives came to Yellville to attend the proceeding. One of George's brothers arrived from Indiana, where the Watkinses and Barkhimers had lived at the time of George and Rebecca's marriage around 1870, and George's father and another brother traveled from Kansas, where George and Rebecca may have lived briefly before moving to Arkansas. The trial, however, was postponed when the judge granted Hudspeth a change of venue to neighboring Boone County.

In October of 1887, a vest that was thought to have been worn by George Watkins the last time he was seen was found on Greasy Creek. The supposition was seemingly confirmed when a patch on the vest was determined to match a dress belonging to Rebecca Watkins. A search for George Watkins's body was undertaken in the Greasy Creek area but to no avail.

Also in October, Rebecca Watkins, who was still being held as a state witness, was released from custody and immediately rearrested on a warrant charging her as an accessory to the murder of her husband. She was incarcerated in the county jail or "old stony," as it was sometimes called, to await the action of a grand jury.

In late December, she was moved from an upstairs cell to a downstairs one, exchanging places with a male prisoner who had removed a stone from the downstairs wall in an attempt to dig his way out. A few days later, Rebecca soaked with coal oil some timbers near the hole where the stone had been, apparently intending to burn her way out. The two jailbirds were then moved back to their original cells and a guard placed on them at night.

In exchange for leniency in her own case, Rebecca was again made a state witness at her former paramour's trial in late January of 1888 at Harrison. She repeated much the same testimony she had given at the preliminary hearing almost a year earlier, and Hudspeth was convicted of first-degree murder and sentenced to hang on April 19. After the proceeding, Rebecca was released from custody, and some observers suggested that, even if the grand jury indicted her, the prosecuting attorney would nol-pros the case. Young Isaiah Watkins was taken in by his father's Kansas relatives.

Rebecca was returned to jail in early March when she was unable to give bond. Soon afterward, she became ill and was moved to the jailer's residence. Although under the care of a doctor, she continued to languish for the next month. She took another turn for the worse in late April and began speaking incoherently as she neared death's door. Her father was summoned from Boone County when it became clear she would not recover. He arrived on the evening of April 25 and was her only relative present during her last hours. She died during the wee hours of the following morning from complications of rheumatism and other diseases and was buried later the same day at the Jefferson Cemetery, west of Yellville.

Meanwhile, Hudspeth's lawyers appealed his conviction to the Arkansas Supreme Court. The high court agreed in late

March to hear the attorneys' motion for a new trial in June, thereby postponing Hudspeth's date with eternity.

Hudspeth's attorneys advanced two lines of argument as the basis of their appeal. The first pertained to several technicalities surrounding the indictment that had been destroyed by fire. One of the specific arguments was that, as a result of the first indictment, Hudspeth was confined in jail at the time of the second indictment and had, therefore, been denied the right to object to the selection of William T. Dobbs, who had been a witness against him at the first hearing, as a member of the second jury. The court, however, disallowed this and all other arguments pertaining to Hudspeth's duplicate indictments.

A second line of argument concerned the character of the state's chief witness, Rebecca Watkins. At the trial, Hudspeth's lawyers had called Andy's brother, J. F. Hudspeth, who had known Rebecca ever since she had moved to Marion County seven years earlier, to testify as to her general reputation in the community for truth and morality. He said her reputation was bad. When the defendant's lawyers asked the witness whether, taking into consideration her reputation, he would believe her under oath, the state objected, and the trial judge upheld the objection. The Supreme Court, however, ruled that the witness should have been allowed to answer the question, and on June 30, 1888, it ordered a new trial on the basis of this error.

Andy Hudspeth, though, apparently didn't want to take his chances with a new trial. Before it could begin, he escaped from the Boone County jail by picking a lock. He was reportedly spotted in Marion County in August, but evidently no attempt was made to apprehend him. A year later, in August of 1889, he was again spotted, this time along the Arkansas River. The Boone County sheriff was dispatched to arrest him and bring him back, but Hudspeth reportedly fled the area a few minutes before the officer arrived.

He was finally recaptured in 1892 in Johnson County,

where he had been living for some time under the alias of J. W. Taylor. He was brought back to Harrison, and his retrial on the Watkins murder charge was held in late July. Despite the fact that the state's star witness, Rebecca Watkins, was long since dead, Hudspeth was again convicted and sentenced to hang.

The execution was set for October 3, but a series of appeals and stays of execution postponed the fateful date until late December. Although Hudspeth had never been a member of any church, on the early morning of his execution day, December 30, he called for a local minister, who visited him in his cell. The condemned man, whose health was failing, said he was ready to die and was praying for all, even those who had "sworn away his life." A newspaper reporter and one of Hudspeth's lawyers also visited the prisoner in jail, and he told his attorney he didn't blame the law officers or any of the court officials. He reasserted his innocence but, as he had from the beginning, refused to discuss the crime further.

Boone County sheriff D. A. Eoff waited all day to see whether there might be a commutation or another stay of execution, but when none was forthcoming, Hudspeth was finally marched to the scaffold about 4:15 in the afternoon. The prisoner mounted the platform "as steadily as could have been expected of one in such feeble health." No friends or relatives were present to comfort him as he was prepared for the execution, and he declined an invitation to speak any final words.

At 4:30, the rope was adjusted around his neck and the door sprung. He dropped to his death and hung without so much as a twitch, his neck having been broken by the fall. After twelve minutes, Hudspeth was pronounced dead and his body cut down. It was then taken by wagon and buried in a local cemetery.

Even at the time of Hudspeth's execution, a few observers questioned the justice of hanging a person for the murder of a man whose body had never been found. Then in late June of 1893, the case took a strange turn when a report came out of Fayetteville that George Watkins had been found alive and well, living on a farm in Kansas.

The report, however, was quickly dismissed as a hoax by folks around Yellville when a local citizen wrote to George Watkins's brother-in-law, who lived in the same vicinity where George was reported to be living, and the relative wrote back stating emphatically that George was not living there and that the family had not seen him since before his disappearance in late 1886. The brother-in-law's assertion, of course, is supported by the fact that the Watkins family had attended Andy Hudspeth's murder trial. If they had had the slightest suspicion that George was still alive, they surely would not have let an innocent man die for his murder. And if George Watkins were alive, he surely would have made an attempt to see Isaiah or contact family members about his son's welfare. One observer suggested that the claim was meant to influence the Arkansas governor to pardon certain individuals around Fayetteville who, like Hudspeth, had been convicted on circumstantial evidence.

It seems logical to conclude, based on the testimony of Rebecca Watkins and her son and on the strong circumstantial evidence, that Andy Hudspeth did, in fact, kill George Watkins. However, the myth that George was later found alive is still perpetuated today, particularly by groups who are opposed to capital punishment or are otherwise campaigning against abuses in the justice system. For instance, Andrew J. Hudspeth, although misidentified as Charles Hudspeth, is listed on the Web site of the Northwestern University School of Law's Center for Wrongful Convictions as someone who was executed for murder and whose supposed victim was later found alive. It would be heartrending if it were true. That miscarriages of justice have occurred in the past and still do on occasion is irrefutable, but the case of Andy Hudspeth likely wasn't one of them.

10

The Exciting Pastime of Shooting
at One Another

On the night of Tuesday, December 3, 1889, Butler, Missouri, city marshal J. H. Morgan and Deputy U.S. Marshal John P. Willis engaged in what one area newspaper called "the exciting pastime of shooting at one another," resulting in the death of both lawmen. An Associated Press dispatch sent out across the country from Kansas City the next day claimed that Morgan was a moonshiner of "desperate reputation," that the confrontation occurred while Willis was attempting to arrest Morgan on a charge of selling liquor without a license, and that Morgan fired a shot at Willis before the deputy marshal returned fire. The Kansas City newspapers reported the incident in much the same manner, except the *Kansas City Globe* suggested that the "tough customer" Morgan got off three shots before Willis was able to return fire, while the *Kansas City Star* said vaguely that Morgan fired "several" times before Willis could draw his pistol and shoot back. Both papers agreed that Willis died instantly and Morgan lingered for several hours.

The local newspapers told a much different story. A headline in the *Bates County Record* reported that City Marshal Morgan was "shot to death like a dog," and another accused Willis of "murder most foul." Saying that there was "not one line of truth" in the *Star* account, that it was a "journalistic outrage," and that "the *Kansas City Globe* was even worse," the *Butler Daily Democrat* concluded that the Kansas City newspapers had "perverted the truth beyond the limit of the least shadow of a reasonable excuse."

In this case, the local press was much closer to the truth of the matter than the metropolitan papers. Not only were the *Kansas City Globe* and the *Kansas City Star* wrong in many details about the encounter, but they were also wrong in blaming Morgan.

The fifty-three-year-old Morgan had been city marshal of Butler for about ten years, was widely considered "the best marshal Butler ever had," and "always had a kind word for everyone." The thirty-eight-year-old Willis had also lived near Butler for ten years or more and had, at one time, run a grocery and dry-goods store. In his thirties, he had been appointed a deputy U.S. marshal. Like Morgan, he was said to be an efficient officer with "many good traits," except that he was also considered, at least by some, to be a hard drinker. There was reputed to be bad blood between Morgan and Willis, dating from an incident in 1882 in which Marshal Morgan, during the legal performance of his duties, had killed a man named John Stanley. A jury found Morgan blameless, and the community also supported the city marshal, but Willis, apparently an acquaintance of Stanley, reportedly held a grudge.

During the late afternoon of December 2, 1889, Willis appeared on the streets of Butler in a state of intoxication and began trying to pick fights and otherwise making himself obnoxious. Constable Charley Lewis happened along and tried to get Willis off the street. Instead, Willis accosted a prominent citizen of Butler named John W. Hannah and reportedly started "abusing both him and his family in the most shameful manner, using the most obscene and insulting language, accompanied by terrible oaths and an occasional thrust of his right hand behind him, as if to show he would draw his revolver if necessary."

Finally Hannah, who had served as an officer in the Confederate army, had enough, and he struck Willis on the head with his cane, knocking the deputy marshal down. Rising, Willis continued his boisterous talk but did not lay into Hannah again. Instead, he saw Marshal Morgan approaching and went to meet him. Willis seemed friendly enough, according to Morgan's own later testimony, until he realized that the city marshal meant to arrest him. Remonstrating, Willis was dragged off to the city jail and lodged in the calaboose. He was let out about two and a half hours later, after he gave a $200 bond promising to keep the peace and to appear for trial the following Saturday.

Still smarting from the humiliation of being arrested, Willis, accompanied by a prominent local attorney named S. P. Francisco, took the early train to Kansas City the next day, December 3, and went to the office of U.S. District Attorney George A. Neal He swore out a complaint charging that Morgan and Hannah had assaulted him while he was performing his official duties as a deputy U.S. marshal. Willis claimed he had a warrant for the arrest of a murderer from No Man's Land whom he suspected was aboard a train scheduled to stop in Butler the previous afternoon. He was getting ready to serve the papers when he was attacked by Morgan and Hannah, with one holding him while the other beat him.

Neal referred the case to U.S. Commissioner W. V. Childs, who swore out warrants against Morgan and Hannah, and Willis promptly started back to Butler with them. At the train depot in Kansas City, he met S. S. Price, an insurance-company representative with whom he had recently been associated in business. Willis deputized Price for the purpose of helping him serve the warrants, and the two men resumed the journey to Butler together. On the trip down, a porter heard Willis making threats toward Morgan and, when the train reached Butler about 9:30 Tuesday night, the porter reportedly tried, in vain, to send warning to the city marshal.

Willis and Price went briefly to a local hotel and then on

to Morgan's former house, where they knocked on the door, arousing the occupants. Informed that Morgan now lived across the street, they went to the indicated house and once again rapped on the door. Morgan asked from the interior of the house, "Who is there?"

Getting no response, he picked up his revolver and went to the door. When he opened it, he saw the two men standing on either side of the door, each holding a pistol. "What do you want?" Morgan asked.

"We've come to arrest you," Willis informed him.

"Where's your warrant?" the city marshal asked.

"It makes no difference about the warrant," Willis reportedly said.

He and Morgan both raised their weapons and fired at about the same time, and each one's bullet struck the other in the abdomen. Willis and Price dragged Morgan from the house into the yard, where the two wounded men struggled over their weapons, with Willis on top of Morgan. Standing a few feet back, Price took no part in the wrestling match except to urge his partner to "shoot him again!"

Willis fired three more shots at the prostrate Morgan As the struggle continued, Mrs. Morgan rushed to the door shrieking, "Murder!" and begging that her husband be spared.

"See here—you hush," Price said threateningly as he pointed his gun in her direction.

As Mrs. Morgan ran next door for help, Willis kept beating her husband about the face and head with his pistol until Morgan collapsed. Mrs. Morgan soon returned with help, and other neighbors, alerted by the shots, quickly arrived on the scene as well. The critically wounded Morgan was taken into his house. Willis was led away but made it only about three hundred feet before he fell and was carried the rest of the way home. Both men lingered throughout the night and into the next day, and both gave statements on their deathbeds.

Gravestone of John P. Willis at Oak Hill Cemetery in Butler.

In his dying statement, Morgan claimed that Willis came to his house not to arrest him but with the express purpose of trying to kill him. His version of events was corroborated not only by his wife but also by neighbors who saw Willis straddle a prostrate Morgan and strike him with his pistol, who overheard Price urging Willis to "shoot him again," and who saw and heard the gunfire when Willis followed through on his partner's suggestion. Willis, however, disclaimed any design to do Morgan bodily harm in obtaining the warrant and going to his house late at night to serve it. After he was arrested as an accomplice and placed in jail the day after the incident, Price, too, gave a statement, emphasizing that he took no part in the shooting and that he only accompanied Willis at the latter's request.

Doctors thought at first that Willis's wound might not prove fatal, but he died about three o'clock in the afternoon on December 4, a couple of hours after Morgan. A coroner's jury convened the same day and found that Willis had been shot once in the abdomen and that Morgan had been shot once in the abdomen and a second time in the right leg. An inspection of the lawmen's weapons revealed that Morgan's revolver had been fired only once and Willis's pistol four times.

Both men were buried the next day, December 5. The mayor of Butler issued a proclamation calling on all businesses to close their doors as a gesture of respect for the dead city marshal, and almost the whole town turned out for Morgan's burial in the early afternoon. (An official memorial service was also held a few days later.) Willis's interment in the late afternoon drew a much smaller crowd, mostly family and close friends of the deceased.

Like the combatants themselves, the people involved in issuing the warrants tried to shift blame once they learned the result of Willis's attempt to serve the writ on Morgan. Childs, the commissioner who issued the warrants, said he did so on the advice of District Attorney Neal. Neal said he at first suggested that the issuing of the warrants be postponed until he could investigate the case but that he finally relented partly at the urging of Mr. Francisco, the attorney who accompanied Willis and who, according to Neal, seemed to be acting as Willis's legal advisor. Francisco, though, said he knew of the bad blood that existed between Willis and Morgan and advised against issuing the warrants to Willis. Childs added that he only issued the warrants with the understanding that they would be handed over to Elijah Gates, U.S. marshal for the Western District of Missouri, and that Gates would, in turn, give them to Deputy Marshal Dennis Malloy to be served rather than Willis, since he was personally involved in the case. Gates said that he asked Willis who had the warrants and that Willis assured him he had handed them over to Malloy. After the shooting, Willis said he had, in fact, asked Malloy to accompany him to Butler but that Malloy took sick and couldn't make the trip. Malloy, though, said the reason he didn't come to Butler was that he preferred to work alone and Willis refused to let him serve the warrant on his own.

After sifting through all the charges and countercharges, a special grand jury impaneled on December 12 came to the conclusion that J. P. Willis committed first-degree murder and that S. S. Price should be charged as an accessory for aiding and abetting the murder. Price, appearing before the Bates County Court on the thirteenth, pled not guilty and was remanded to the Henry County jail in Clinton to await trial.

A few small-town area newspapers joined the *Butler Daily Democrat* and *Bates County Record* in condemning the erroneous accounts by the Kansas City papers and the Associated Press. The *Lamar Missourian*, for instance, stated indignantly that it should not have been possible for a marshal who had been on "a howling drunk" for several days to obtain official papers "to gratify personal malice," but that is what Willis apparently did. Because of such editorial criticism and the public outcry of Bates County citizens, a few newspapers, such as the *Fort Scott Monitor*, which had printed the Associated Press account of the killings, issued retractions, but the Kansas City papers, despite the evidence to the contrary, largely stood by their initial reports.

11

Olyphant: The Last Great Arkansas Train Robbery

At noon on November 3, 1893, veteran conductor William P. McNally and 300 passengers left Poplar Bluff, Missouri, aboard Train No. 51 bound for Texarkana, Arkansas, by way of Little Rock, on the St. Louis, Iron Mountain and Southern Railway. A longtime railroad man who was nearing retirement, the fifty-two-year-old McNally had made the 300-mile run many times, and he looked forward to this trip as one of his last. He didn't count on it being his very last.

After halting for dinner at Walnut Creek, the train took off again about 7:30. It stopped at Olyphant, a small village seven miles south of the Jackson County seat of Newport, shortly before 10:00 to let off a single passenger. After the passenger disembarked, the seven-car train pulled onto a siding to let the high-speed northbound "Cannonball" pass.

Train 51 had scarcely come to a halt on the side track when seven masked bandits suddenly charged out of the cold, rainy darkness to surround the engine. (The outlaw gang consisted of eight men, but the eighth member was left to guard the bandits' horses in a nearby canebrake.) Brandishing their Winchesters, the robbers covered engineer Robert Herriott and fireman John Quarles and shouted for them to throw up their hands. The pair did as they were told.

The outlaw gang had formed several weeks earlier in the Benton County vicinity of northwest Arkansas, where most of the desperadoes lived. James Wyrick, Tom Brady, and George

Padgett had gotten together in nearby Indian Territory, where one or more of them had been smuggling and selling whiskey, and the three men began bandying about the idea of holding up a train as a get-rich-quick scheme. Ol Truman, Bob Chesney, and brothers Sam and Pennyweight Powell, all of whom were apparently just farmers from the Siloam Springs area with little or no criminal history, were recruited shortly afterward. The three ringleaders rode east around the first of October to scout out the St. Louis, Iron Mountain and Southern Railway line. Padgett, a former Little Rock policeman, took a ride on Train 51 in late October and learned that it stopped at Olyphant to drop off mail and to allow another train to pass. He also discovered that, over the next several days, the train would be carrying a number of wealthy passengers home from the Chicago World's Fair, so he and his sidekicks decided on Train 51 as their target. At some point during their sojourn, the desperadoes hooked up in Howell County, Missouri, with Albert Mansker, who had previous experience in the work of train robbery and welcomed the prospect of pulling off another job.

About three weeks after leaving home, Wyrick returned to Benton County to get the other four members of the gang. Wyrick, Truman, Chesney, and the Powell brothers told their families that they were going to look for a site to start a lumberyard, and they started out in a wagon loaded with Winchesters and ammunition and leading two horses. Around the end of October, the eight outlaws rendezvoused in Jamestown, a small town about thirty-five miles northwest of Olyphant, where they stayed on the property of H. H. Wackerly, with whom some of the gang were apparently acquainted. From Jamestown, the gang rode to a rural church about three miles from Olyphant, where they drank whiskey to bolster their courage before riding on to the railroad station.

Now, with the engineer and fireman under arrest, three of the bandits started marching the prisoners toward the express car, while four of the gang, two on either side of the train, maintained a lookout. The outlaw threesome ordered their captives to open the express car, but Herriott told them he was unable to do so. The highwaymen then shouted for the express messenger to open up, and they started shooting at the door when he did not immediately obey their command. He then quickly complied, but the four lookouts kept pelting the train with lead and punctuating their gunfire with loud oaths to intimidate the passengers. All told, an estimated one hundred to two hundred shots were fired at the train. Entering the express car, the three ringleaders forced the express messenger at gunpoint to open the safe, and the bandits quickly emptied the strongbox of its contents.

Toward the back of the train, Conductor McNally heard the commotion, and a baggage attendant rushed up and told him it was a holdup. McNally hurried through the passenger cars, warning travelers to hide their valuables. Borrowing a pistol from passenger Charles Lamb, McNally then stepped out onto the platform of the baggage car, followed by the baggage man, and opened fire at the gang. The bandits promptly returned fire. McNally, struck in the abdomen, sank back into the arms of the baggage attendant and died almost instantly. The dying man tried to ask bystanders who rushed to the scene to relay a message to his sister but expired before he could finish giving her name and address. Lamb, meanwhile, managed to secure another weapon and also opened fire on the outlaws. The gang poured a barrage of lead in the shooter's direction, but Lamb, miraculously untouched by the hail of bullets, ceased fire only because his gun malfunctioned.

After emptying out the express safe, the three ringleaders turned their attention to the passenger cars. Marching the engineer and fireman ahead of them as hostages, the robbers swept through the cars collecting all of the valuables and money that the travelers had not been able to conceal after McNally's warning. At some point, the train's porter was also forced to join the parade through the cars. One bandit gathered the loot while the other two trailed behind him, keeping the prisoners and passengers covered. The engineer described the one collecting the goods, who later was thought to be Padgett, as a slender man about five feet ten inches tall, while a passenger claimed he was "a vicious, blood-thirsty-look fellow, at least six feet four inches tall."

According to some of the passengers, the outlaws announced that they only wanted contributions from those who were able to give and that they would not target ladies or workingmen. However, they "did not strictly adhere to the policy announced," according to one observer, because "several workingmen lost all they had while others were not molested." Estimates of the robbers' take vary widely, but the total lifted from the express safe and stolen from the passengers was probably in the neighborhood of two or three thousand dollars.

Leon L. Lippman, a local sawmill owner who had come to the station to meet Train 51, realized what was taking place. As the Cannonball approached Olyphant, Lippman grabbed a red lantern and waved it to flag down the passing train. The engineer of the northbound Cannonball mistook the frantic signal as an all-clear sign and went speeding by.

After plundering the passenger cars, ending with the sleeper at the rear of the train, the three robbers strode back through the cars toward the front, still herding their prisoners ahead of them. One of the gang bid the travelers in one of the cars a "good night" as he passed through. When the bandits got back to the train's engine, they stood their captives in front of its headlight so that they could keep an eye on the railroad men while they retrieved their horses. Then, they mounted up, bid the hostages good night, and galloped west into the dank night.

It was about 10:20 as the bandits rode away, the robbery having consumed approximately thirty-five minutes. News of the holdup was immediately telegraphed to railroad officials and law-enforcement officers throughout the region. By eleven o'clock, Sheriff James Hobgood of Jackson County

and his deputies were "in hot pursuit" of the bandits, and
two other posses, including one organized by private citizen
Lippman, soon joined in the chase. Fifteen hunting dogs were
also secured, and "in less than two hours after the robbery,"
according to one report, "the canebrakes about Oliphant
were ringing with the sounds of baying bloodhounds on the
trail of the bandits."

Meanwhile, less than an hour after the holdup, Train No. 51
went on to Little Rock, carrying its passengers and McNally's
body. The next day, the dead conductor's sister was identified,
and his remains were shipped to her in Cleveland, Ohio.

News of the killing of McNally, who was well known all
along the line of the St. Louis, Iron Mountain and Southern
railroad, was met with outrage throughout Arkansas and
southeastern Missouri, and both railroad officials and the
governor of Arkansas offered rewards for the arrest of the
perpetrators. The story of the robbery made front-page
headlines in the *Arkansas Gazette* and other regional papers
and stirred citizens to a fever of excitement. The *Gazette*
continued to chronicle the chase after the fugitives over the
next several days as readers eagerly awaited the latest word on
the sensational story. Speculation swirled as to the identity of
the robbers, and one report even claimed that the holdup
had been carried out by the Dalton gang.

The posses formed at Olyphant in the immediate wake
of the robbery struck the trail of the bandits shortly after
midnight and pursued them in a northwesterly direction
toward Batesville. By daylight on Saturday, November 4,
lawmen and civilians from miles around, totalling nearly
a hundred men, had joined in the chase. That afternoon,
acting on a tip that several "suspicious strangers" had
been seen hanging around the Wackerly home during the
past week or so, the posses closed in on the fugitives near
Jamestown.

A posse consisting of Woodruff County sheriff Marshall
Patterson, Independence County deputy sheriff Oscar
Pennington, and Mr. Lippman caught up with two of the

gang about five o'clock Saturday afternoon a couple of miles west of Jamestown. Carrying only concealed pistols, the lawmen engaged the two heavily armed men in ordinary conversation and were able to disarm them before the fugitives realized the identity of the newcomers. Taken back to the Independence County seat at Batesville, the captives were identified as two of the train robbers due to their possession of valuables stolen from passengers and a handdrawn map of the robbers' planned escape route from the Olyphant station through the Boston Mountains to Indian Territory. But the prisoners refused to give their names. Later, one of them, described as about five feet ten inches tall, said he was Mack Arnett, while his partner, a small man barely over five feet, identified himself as Bill Lemons.

Ironically, a railroad employee named J. R. Lemons was arrested the same day in Little Rock on suspicion of being in complicity with the robbers. Speculation abounded that the two men were brothers, but that theory quickly proved not to be the case, and J. R. Lemons was exonerated. Over the next several weeks, numerous other men throughout northern Arkansas were, like J. R. Lemons, temporarily detained as "suspicious characters" or for "knowing too much" about the robbery before being proven innocent.

Late Saturday night, scores of lawmen continued to scour the countryside of Independence County for the remaining robbers, with Batesville now serving as the base of operations for the intensifying manhunt. Jamestown postmaster M. C. Long assembled a posse of local men, and H. H. Wackerly's sons, twenty-two-year-old John and nineteen-year-old Clem, were recruited to join the party, even though they were suspected of knowing more about the train robbery than they had revealed. After beating the bush on foot all night, the posse came upon several armed men on horseback about daylight Sunday morning near Long's home. One of the strangers turned to his partners and warned them to "look out," and the gang galloped off. Long fired a shotgun blast at the riders, knocking the hat off one of them, but they made their escape with no serious injuries. During the brief skirmish, Clem Wackerly threw down his weapon and ran off. He was later captured but escaped and fled to Conway, Arkansas, where he was shot and recaptured after a showdown with lawmen and then held on suspicion of being in cahoots with the train robbers.

On Thursday night, November 9, almost a week after the robbery, a third bandit was caught near Snowball in Searcy County, Arkansas. He gave his name as Jim Williams and was taken back to Batesville. Meanwhile, the men calling themselves Arnett and Lemons were transported to the state penitentiary at Little Rock, and the newest captive soon joined them.

Around the fourteenth of November, most of the gang members were tentatively identified based on reports filtering in from Benton County and other evidence gathered from various sources by law-enforcement officers. A few days later, the identity of the two bandits arrested at Jamestown was confirmed when two citizens of Benton County, who had traveled to Little Rock for a Masonic meeting, were allowed to view the train robbers at the penitentiary and testified that Lemons was none other than Benton County farmer Tom Brady and that Arnett was really George Padgett, a resident of Indian Territory who was known in the Benton County area. About the same time, the five Benton County residents still at large—Wyrick, Truman, Chesney, and the Powell brothers—were also named as definite participants in the crime.

The true identity of the man calling himself Jack Williams remained a mystery, however. A few days after the other seven robbers had been positively identified, "Williams" said he was really Albert Mansker from the Howell County, Missouri, area. It was later asserted that the man was actually James Hill of Mammoth Spring, Arkansas (just across the border from Howell County). The robber himself, however, never withdrew his claim to be Albert Mansker, and even to this day a disagreement persists among family historians as to whether the eighth Olyphant train robber was Albert Mansker or James Hill.

The four principal Olyphant train robbers. (Courtesy Jacksonport State Park)

In early December, Wyrick was captured near Van Buren in Crawford County, Arkansas by a posse led by a railroad detective. The prisoner was transported directly to the penitentiary at Little Rock. By Christmas, Chesney and the Powell brothers had also been apprehended, and Truman was captured later.

The trials for the ringleaders of the gang were set to begin in late January of 1894 in Newport, and circuit judge James W. Butler ruled that anyone convicted of the robbery would also be accountable for McNally's death. George Padgett, however, agreed to cooperate with authorities in exchange for leniency, and he was not tried for murder, even though the testimony of witnesses and other evidence suggested that he was the robber who had gathered the loot from the passengers and was one of the leaders of the gang.

In the separate trials of Brady and Wyrick held in late January, Padgett was the main witness against them, testifying that the two men came to him with the idea of robbing a train and that meetings were later held with Albert Mansker. The train's brakeman testified that Wyrick was the man who fired the shot that killed McNally. Wyrick admitted he was in on the original scheme, but he claimed he got drunk and left the group before the actual robbery. The court was not swayed by such a flimsy alibi. Both Wyrick and Brady were convicted of first-degree murder and scheduled to hang on April 6 in Newport.

Mansker (or Hill) claimed he was the one who had held the gang's horses during the train holdup. Still, some considered him the ringleader of the group, probably because he had been involved in previous robberies, and they said he had talked the others into going through with the crime. At his trial in early February, he, too, was convicted of murder in the first degree and slated to join his two partners on the gallows.

Indictments were later brought against Truman, Chesney, and the Powell brothers, but they were never brought to trial (although one of the Powell brothers was charged and found guilty of a previous minor crime). The people were apparently satisfied that the main instigators and perpetrators had been held to account.

Appeals for all three condemned men were made to the Arkansas Supreme Court and Gov. William Fishback but were turned down. On the night of April 5, 1894, several women visited the convicts in the Jackson County jail at Newport to sing hymns and to join Mansker and Wyrick in praying for Brady, who refused to accept religion. The next morning, however, according to one report, "all the condemned were praying" as they were led onto the scaffold. A large crowd estimated at nearly a thousand people had gathered for the event, but only twenty-five witnesses were allowed inside an enclosure surrounding the gallows. The men were given an opportunity to make final statements. All three proclaimed their innocence or suggested that "drink

Scene at the triple execution of Brady, Mansker, and Wyrick. (Courtesy Jacksonport State Park)

and bad company" had led to their downfall and that George Padgett had been the main instigator of the crime. Moments later, with their protestations of innocence still on their lips, the three men dropped to their deaths in the only triple execution in Jackson County history.

12

The Meadows-Bilyeu Feud:
A Pitched and Bloody Battle

The day after John "Bud" Meadows killed Steve Bilyeu and two of his sons on Bull Creek fifteen miles south of Ozark, Missouri, on November 28, 1898, the *Springfield Leader Democrat* called the incident "a pitched and bloody battle" and said that it was the "most fatal culmination of a

TUESDAY EVENING--SPRING

IS AN AWFUL FEUD.

A Pitched and Bloody Battle on Christian and Taney Counties Border.

Steve Bilyeu and His Two Sons Are Killed, While a Son-In-Law Is Badly Wounded—Ill Feeling For Years.

Springfield newspaper headline describing the Bilyeu-Meadows showdown.

neighborhood feud in the history of Christian County." The same report stated the tragedy was "the most bloody affair that has ever happened on Bull Creek," an area that, the *Democrat* pointed out, had been "long ago noted for its deadly feuds."

All of this was true enough, except that the dispute was more of a family feud than a neighborhood feud. As a Kansas newspaper noted a few months later, the Meadows and Bilyeu families were "so united by intermarriage that it is hard to pick out a certain member of either and say with any degree of exactness just what he or she is."

The squabble that finally erupted into violence on that late autumn day had been brewing for at least a year. The thirty-year-old Meadows and the fifty-three-year-old Bilyeu owned farms adjoining each other on the west side of Bull Creek near the Taney County line, and they started out as friends. Bud Meadows was married to a daughter of Hosea Bilyeu, who was a first cousin of Steve Bilyeu and had been raised in Steve's family almost like a brother. Bud's brother, Robert "Bob" Meadows, had also married into the Bilyeu family. Several years earlier, Bud and Steve had put up a common fence separating their properties, with each contributing materials and labor to the project. But in the fall of 1897, as the fence began to deteriorate from age, a rift developed between the two men over its upkeep. Meadows told Bilyeu he wasn't holding up his end of the bargain, but Bilyeu dismissed the complaint without doing any repair on the fence.

When Meadows approached Bilyeu a second time in the spring of 1898, he was again rebuffed and, according to his own story, decided to seek legal redress. Consulting a lawyer at Ozark, Meadows drew up an affidavit, dated May 4, 1898, informing Bilyeu that six months from that date he intended to remove his part of the joint fence. This action infuriated Bilyeu, and during the next several months, according to legend, several confrontations occurred over the issue of the fence. In one incident, for instance, twenty-six-year-old Pete Bilyeu, Steve's son, supposedly threatened Bud Meadows with a revolver and made him crawl on the ground. Another time, as the Bilyeus walked away from a confrontation at the fence, Frank Tabor, who was married to a daughter of Steve's but was siding with Bud in the dispute, reportedly crowed like a rooster to express his disdain at their retreat.

In early November of 1898, when the official notice Meadows had drawn up expired, he went to the fence with a gun and an ax, intending to start taking it down. He was met, however, by Steve and Pete Bilyeu, both of whom were armed. Hurling threats and abuse, they forced him to lay down his gun and ax and to leave.

The fence in question, starting near the home of Bud Meadows, ran east for approximately fifty yards, turned south for about two hundred yards, and then east for another fifty yards or so. Shortly after the confrontation in early November, the Bilyeus removed the north-south section of the fence, but by the latter part of the month, the two east-west sections remained.

On the morning of November 28, several of Meadows's neighbors, including his brother Bob, Frank Tabor, and Hosea Bilyeu, arrived at Bud's place to help him take down the rest of the fence. Bud and his brother began work at the west end near the Meadows house, while the other hands went to work removing the east end of the fence, setting aside the poles and riders that belonged to Bilyeu and reserving for Meadows the rails that he had contributed to the joint project. While they were thus engaged, Steve and Pete Bilyeu came to the east end of the fence around noon, armed and driving a wagon for the purpose of hauling away the posts and rails. The Bilyeus cursed and threatened the workers and told them to leave the fence alone.

Hearing the commotion, Bud Meadows went into his house and retrieved his Winchester rifle, his brother's shotgun, and Hosea Bilyeu's pistol, and he and Bob started toward the scene of the altercation. On the way, they saw Steve Bilyeu's wife, Elizabeth, and the couple's sixteen-year-old son, James Bilyeu, hurrying toward the scene as well, with the boy carrying a revolver. When they got to the east section of the fence, according to Bud's own account of the incident, Steve Bilyeu claimed the fence was his and "threatened to kill any damned son of a bitch that touched a rail."

After arguing with Bilyeu awhile, Meadows finally agreed to leave the fence alone for the time being but said that he would reclaim the rails through court action if necessary. Telling his workers to come with him to the west end of the fence, he turned and started away.

As Bud was walking away, someone yelled for him to look out, and when he turned back around, Steve Bilyeu was aiming his shotgun at him. Steve fired but missed. Meadows raised his Winchester and returned fire, also missing the mark. He fired a second time, though, killing Bilyeu instantly. Bob Meadows and Pete Bilyeu also exchanged errant shots, and as the latter was getting ready to fire again, Bud shifted his aim toward Pete and brought him down with his Winchester.

Mrs. Bilyeu charged toward Bud Meadows with a butcher knife and slashed him several times. Jim Bilyeu was standing nearby with his revolver, trying to get a shot at Bud, but he was afraid of hitting his mother. He yelled for her to get away, but before she could, Bud aimed his rifle over her shoulder and dropped the boy in his tracks. The distraught Elizabeth Bilyeu rushed to her fallen husband and sons, but she found all three of them already dead.

Bud's version of what happened as related above is a composite of what he told a Springfield newspaper the day after the battle and what he maintained during his subsequent legal fight. Not surprisingly, it differs considerably from the Bilyeu side of the story. The Bilyeu side, however, did not receive the publicity that Bud's version did, mainly because there were few potential witnesses left alive to tell the victims' side. Those who did testify on behalf of the Bilyeus, though, claimed it was Bud Meadows who fired first.

According to the Bilyeu side of the story, Bud was walking

away after the argument over the rails when his wife, Salina, called to him from some distance away, urging her husband to fight. "Kill them, Bud," she shouted, "or die for your rights! Do not let them steal your labor."

Meadows turned and, upon seeing Steve Bilyeu in the act of picking up a rail, shot and killed him, and Steve's gun discharged accidentally. The Bilyeus also claimed that Bob Meadows shot Pete first, disabling him, before Bud finished him off with a shot in the back of the head and that Hosea Bilyeu, not Bud Meadows, killed young Jim Bilyeu.

Several hours after the shootings, Bud Meadows, Bob Meadows, Hosea Bilyeu, and Hosea's son Martin went to Ozark to turn themselves in, and they were placed in the Christian County jail. Frank Tabor, who had been wounded during the free-for-all and had come to Ozark earlier in the day to have his injuries treated, was also lodged in the calaboose.

The victims of the shootings were buried on December 1 at the Spokane Cemetery in southern Christian County, and a large crowd gathered for the occasion.

Spokane Cemetery, where Jimmy, Pete, and Steve Bilyeu are buried.

All five men accused in the deaths of the Bilyeus were indicted for murder, and Bud Meadows was tried first, at the April 1899 term of the Christian County Circuit Court. Curious spectators swarmed in from the hills and hollows to watch the proceedings, and a parade of witnesses marched to the stand to tell what they knew about the deadly gun battle. One man who claimed to have been present at the fight was asked what he had observed. Injecting a note of somber humor into the trial, he replied that he saw three men shot down but then he left because he "thought there was going to be trouble."

Several witnesses for the defense testified to the bad character of the victims, claiming the Bilyeus were "turbulent and violent and dangerous men." There may have been some truth to this assertion. Pete Bilyeu had a weapons charge and a charge of crippling and maiming a heifer against him in Christian County during the early 1890s, and he and his father were indicted in 1894 for disturbing the peace at a social gathering.

However, Bud Meadows had been implicated in a string of crimes that was at least as lengthy and impressive as that of the Bilyeus. The most serious charge resulted from Bud's involvement in a feud in the Bull Creek country between the Matthews and Payton families during the Bald Knobber era of the 1880s. Bud and his father, Alexander "Old Bob" Meadows, sided with the Paytons in the dispute, and their involvement led to Old Bob being ambushed and shot, supposedly in retaliation for the death of a Matthews child. The child's father was tried and acquitted in the killing of Old Bob. Several years after the fact, Bud Meadows was finally indicted as an accessory in the murder of the Matthews child, but he, too, was tried and acquitted.

No such luck this time! In the April trial of 1899, the jury must have believed that Bud's character was at least as dubious as Bilyeu's, because they convicted him of killing Bilyeu and sentenced him to ten years in the state prison.

He remained in jail at Ozark, however, while awaiting the outcome of an appeal filed by his attorneys.

In July of 1899, Bud's brother Bob went on trial for the shooting death of Pete Bilyeu. He was acquitted after Pete's body was exhumed and an autopsy determined that the victim had been shot in the front of the head, not the back as the Bilyeus claimed.

The next month, Hosea Bilyeu was tried for the murder of Jimmy Bilyeu. He, too, was acquitted, partly on the testimony of Bud Meadows, who appeared as a key defense witness. Bud repeated the story he had told from the beginning: that he alone killed all three victims.

Shortly after Hosea Bilyeu's acquittal, Bud Meadows was released on bond pending the ruling of the Supreme Court on his appeal, and in May of 1900, the high court granted him a new trial. He and his fellow defendants were then re-indicted in August of 1900, but the indictments were dismissed the following December. Thus ended the legal proceedings in the Meadows-Bilyeu feud, but the grudges and resentments lasted for years. Even today, it's easy to find people around Ozark and south of town in the Bull Creek country who have strong feelings about the "bloody battle" on the Christian and Taney counties border. As the Kansas newspaperman suggested over a hundred years ago, though, it's not always easy to tell whether you're talking to a Meadows or Bilyeu, because a lot of the time the person you're talking to is both.

13

The Missouri Kid and the
Union Bank Robbery

In February 1904, twenty-one-year-old William "The Missouri Kid" Rudolph was apprehended for robbing a bank at Union, Missouri, and murdering a Pinkerton agent sent out to arrest him. The *New York Times* would report that Rudolph came from a family of "crackers" living at the "foot of the Ozark mountains in one of the wildest sections of Missouri," suggesting that his primitive upbringing may have shaped his violent and criminal nature. The editor of the hometown *Franklin County Tribune*, however, noted that the mother's family, the Armisteads, although poor, were considered honest and that the kid's stepfather, Frank Rudolph, was an "honest old painter whose chief fault was his love for liquor." Everyone, including the lad's own mother, seemed to agree, though, that Willie Rudolph was "always a bad boy."

William was born in January of 1883 to John Anderson and Nancy Jane Armistead when the mother was just eighteen years old, and there is no record that the couple ever married. About three years later, Nancy married Frank Rudolph, and her son adopted the stepfather's surname, although he was also sometimes known as William Anderson or William Armistead. The boy grew up in Franklin County, living mostly in the southern part, along the Bourbeuse River near Stanton.

When young Rudolph was about sixteen years old, he fell

114

in with some older boys and helped them rob an elderly couple named Schwartz, who lived on Dry Branch not far from Stanton. The gang reportedly tortured the man and his wife with hot irons to try to get them to reveal the whereabouts of a treasure that the hoodlums thought was hidden on the premises. Rudolph was implicated in the crime, but he skipped town rather than face charges and was not heard from again for almost four years. One report says he spent about a year working in the lead mines at Joplin, Missouri, and another suggests that he slipped back home to visit relatives from time to time while staying out of the public eye.

Around December 18, 1902, Willie came home with a companion who introduced himself as Fred Lewis but whose real name was George Collins. The pair hatched a plan to rob the Bank of Union, and Collins, who was about twenty-three years old, visited Union on Christmas Eve to reconnoiter the place. The duo planned to rob the bank that night, but by the time Collins got back to the Rudolph home ten miles southwest of Union to report his findings, the roads were so muddy they decided to postpone the job.

By the afternoon of December 26, the ground had frozen, and Rudolph and Collins started for Union, arriving about midnight. The men went to the bank, located on a corner of the square, and threw sticks at two nearby electric streetlights, knocking them out. After examining the bank and the downtown area to make sure no night watchmen were guarding the premises, they broke the large front window of the bank to gain entrance.

Rudolph, who claimed to have experience with explosives, entered the bank loaded with nitroglycerin, while Collins stood guard outside. When Rudolph blew the vault door shortly after one o'clock, Collins commenced a random gunfire outside the bank to disguise the explosion. The ruse apparently worked, as many townspeople mistook the noise as fireworks from revelers belatedly celebrating Christmas.

A few citizens living in the immediate vicinity of the bank suspected what was happening, but Collins warned them off with gunfire that pelted their residence if they dared venture out or even turned on a light. Oscar Busch, for instance, who lived above his hardware store across the street from the bank, was awakened by the explosion and went to his front window to look out. As he started to open the window, Collins fired a volley of lead in his direction and yelled at him "in no uncertain tone or language" to stay in the house. Two other men went so far as to arm themselves with shotguns and venture into the street, but because their guns were loaded with fine shot, they "deemed it the safest plan to make no hostile demonstration but watch the pyrotechnic display from a distance."

It took Rudolph about fifteen minutes from the time he blew open the vault door to fix a second charge and blow open the safe. The second explosion confirmed the suspicions of the curious, but by now it was too late. Rudolph quickly emerged from the bank toting a large bag containing about twelve thousand dollars in gold, silver, and paper money, as well as a large amount of bonds and other securities, and he and Collins started east on foot. At the edge of town, they stole a horse and rode it a few miles south before abandoning it. The robbers walked on to St. Clair and headed southwest on the "big road" (which followed roughly the route of present-day I-44) until turning off near Stanton and making their way to the Rudolph home. After a day or two there, they left for Hot Springs, Arkansas, and stayed in the resort town about two weeks before returning to Stanton near the middle of January 1903.

Meanwhile, Pinkerton agent Charles J. Schumacher of St. Louis arrived in Franklin County to aid local authorities in their investigation of the bank robbery. Schumacher's inquiries soon led him to Stanton, where he learned that Willie Rudolph had returned to the area in mid-December after a long absence and that his stepfather, who was known to be destitute, had been spending more money than usual in recent days. On Thursday, January 22, the detective and a companion, disguised as hunters, called at the Rudolph residence, an abandoned boardinghouse for miners about four miles north of Stanton that one report called a "ramshackle affair," and asked for a drink of water and something to eat. Mrs. Rudolph invited them in, and her son calmly told the men to set their guns in a corner. Willie, with two pistols strapped to his waist, positioned himself between his guests and their weapons as his mother served them dinner, and he stayed there throughout their visit.

Schumacher left the home convinced that William Rudolph was one of the men involved in the Union bank robbery, and upon his return to Stanton, he promptly telephoned his suspicion to the sheriff's office at Union. The Franklin County prosecuting attorney immediately swore out a warrant for young Rudolph's arrest for his part in the assault on the Schwartz couple over four years earlier, and Deputy Sheriff Louis Vedder met Schumacher at four o'clock that afternoon in Stanton with the warrant. The detective wanted to proceed at once to the Rudolph home, but Vedder convinced him to wait until morning because it was snowing heavily and darkness was approaching.

About eight o'clock the next morning, January 23, Schumacher, Vedder, and two other men set out from Stanton on foot and arrived at the Rudolph home about two hours later. Vedder knocked at one of the two front doors with Schumacher close behind him and the other two deputies farther back. Suddenly Willie Rudolph and George Collins sprang out from the other door, both with a revolver in each hand, and opened fire. Schumacher seemed to be their target, as he was riddled with bullets, including two shots to the head that killed him instantly. His companions retreated safely to some nearby underbrush, where they exchanged shots with the desperadoes, wounding Collins in the head. Running low on ammunition, the lawmen then withdrew to Stanton to tell what had happened, leaving Schumacher lying dead where he had fallen.

As soon as the deputies left, Rudolph and Collins went back inside the house to dress Collins's wound and clean and reload their weapons. They then crossed the Bourbeuse River and spent the afternoon among Rudolph's kinsmen, trying to secure horses on which to make their getaway.

When news of Schumacher's killing reached Union, a sheriff's posse, reinforced at St. Clair, headed toward the location where the deadly encounter had occurred. When they got close to the scene, the lawmen split up to scour the area.

Meanwhile, the kinfolk had proved less cooperative than Rudolph might have hoped in providing mounts for him and his sidekick to make their getaway, but late in the afternoon Josiah Armistead reluctantly sold the pair two ponies for $200 in gold. The fugitives started southwest and rode only a few minutes before happening upon two of the deputies who were searching the area. Rudolph and Collins ordered the lawmen to halt and throw up their hands. Instead, the deputies opened fire, but the desperadoes returned fire and made their escape.

At the Rudolph home later that day, the posse found Schumacher's body still lying where it had fallen, and it was taken to Stanton and ultimately Chicago for burial. The next day, lawmen returned to the Rudolph home and found a sack of silver taken in the Union bank robbery hidden in a cistern and also found other evidence on the property. The entire Rudolph family, including the stepfather, mother, a sister, and uncle by marriage, were arrested and taken to Union for questioning, but no further trace of the outlaws was found in the area.

Rudolph and Collins, meanwhile, had worked their way southwest to Bourbon, then doubled back east to DeSoto, where they abandoned their horses and hopped a freight train to Memphis. At Memphis, they boarded another train that took them to Collins's hometown of Hartford,

Connecticut, where they felt they would be safe. However, a charred scrap of paper bearing the name "George Collins" was found in a stove at the Rudolph home, soon leading lawmen to Hartford. Pinkerton agents, aided by local police, arrested the fugitives there on March 1, 1903, at a "notorious house" not far from the tenement in which they were staying. Collins and his two half-brothers were arrested on the street as they were exiting the house, while two detectives rushed into Rudolph's room and overpowered him before he could draw his pistol. He put up a fight, though, biting and kicking, before he was subdued. About $2,000 in currency was found on Rudolph's person, while another $6,000 in gold and currency was found in a trunk at the boardinghouse where the two men had been staying. Newspaper stories at the time of their capture called Rudolph "The Missouri Kid" and referred to Collins as "Black Frank." Noting that William Rudolph was "a criminal in looks," the *New York Times* claimed that he and his sidekick had "started in to make dime-novel records in Missouri."

The outlaws were brought back to Union in early March and indicted for first-degree murder in the death of Detective Schumacher. They were then taken to St. Louis for "safekeeping," since the Franklin County jail at Union was not considered secure enough. A large crowd gathered outside the Four Courts jail in St. Louis when Rudolph and Collins were brought in. The desperadoes were reportedly greeted like returning heroes, with the handsome Rudolph, in particular, drawing the attention of some of the young women in the crowd.

The St. Louis facility, though, was apparently not particularly secure either. On July 6, 1903, Rudolph and most of the other prisoners were allowed access during the day to the prison's large central hall. Late in the afternoon, as the guards were returning the inmates to their cells, Rudolph made a daring dash for freedom. While a couple of his fellow prisoners got into a scuffle in another part of the

Photo of William Rudolph from a local newspaper at the time of his arrest.

facility to create a diversion, Rudolph ran up three flights of stairs and, climbing out onto an iron girder that supported the ceiling, reached a skylight. He broke the skylight to gain access to the roof. From there he dropped twenty feet to the chapel roof and then twenty more feet to the ground. He then ran through the jailer's house to the street outside and was quickly out of sight.

His trail was picked up three days later at Mooresville in northwest Missouri, where he hired a team and drove south, but all trace of the escaped killer was lost after that. Upon learning of the escape, William Pinkerton declared, "The world is not big enough to hide Bill Rudolph." But despite a massive manhunt, nothing more was heard from the fugitive for over six months.

Then, on the night of January 16, 1904, Rudolph hooked up with another yeggman named Rogers in the small town of Cleveland, Missouri, about thirty-five miles south of Kansas City. They were getting ready to blow open a bank safe when the cashier discovered them and fired at them with a shotgun. The two burglars ran out of the bank, stole a horse, and fled across the state line to Louisburg, Kansas, a small town on the Missouri, Kansas, and Texas Railroad. Finding the train depot deserted, the two crooks forced open the door and charged the safe with nitroglycerine. They used too much explosive, though, and not only destroyed the contents of the safe but also blew the safe's door clear through the roof. They raced away empty handed and started up the railroad track on foot. They had not gone far, though, when dawn broke the next morning, and a posse of almost two hundred members of the local anti-horse-thief league soon tracked them down. The outlaws took to the brush when they were first sighted but gave up without a fight when the posse surrounded them. They had four big revolvers in their possession when captured and enough nitroglycerin "to blow open twenty safes."

The men were taken to jail at Paola, Kansas. Rogers was then turned over to Missouri authorities on a charge of horse stealing, while Rudolph, who gave his name as Albert Gorney, was charged with attempting to rob the safe at Louisburg. He pled guilty, hoping that, inside the walls of the Kansas prison under an assumed name, he would be safe from discovery by Missouri authorities.

Sentenced to an indeterminate term of five to ten years at the state penitentiary in Lansing, Rudolph arrived there on February 10 and was put to work the next day in the coal mines on the prison grounds. Meanwhile, a photo of the criminal taken at Paola was forwarded to the Pinkerton agency. William Pinkerton recognized it and sent a detective on February 15 to the Kansas prison to make a positive identification. When the inmate was brought to the warden's office, the detective said, "Hi, Bill." The startled "Albert

Gorney" knew he had been found out. Rudolph had pried a couple of gold teeth out of his mouth with a pen knife to try to disguise his appearance, but a photo taken when he was arrested at Hartford and a description of identifying marks on his body that was recorded at the same time were used to confirm the identification.

The governor of Kansas quickly pardoned Rudolph on the burglary conviction so that he could be brought back to Missouri to stand trial for the murder of Detective

Excerpt of letter from William Rudolph to detective William Pinkerton. (Courtesy Library of Congress)

Schumacher. "Thus begins the last act in one of the wildest dramas in the criminal history of this state," noted a Missouri newspaper at the time.

Rudolph's trial for first-degree murder began at Union in late March of 1904. He was in the courthouse for the closing phase of the trial on Saturday, March 26, when Collins was hanged from a gallows in the adjoining jail yard for the same crime Rudolph was being tried for. Two hours later, a jury returned a verdict of guilty in Rudolph's own case. "It's all right," he is reported to have commented. "George is gone; I'd just as soon follow suit."

A series of appeals and reprieves, however, held up Rudolph's execution for over a year, and the condemned man apparently had a change of heart about following suit. As his date with death approached in the spring of 1905, Rudolph wrote two letters from his jail cell to William Pinkerton, pleading with the detective chief to please use his "powerfull influence with the Governor to have my sentence commuted." The final letter, written on May 2, 1905, was received and filed in the Pinkerton office on May 5, three days before Rudolph was scheduled to die. The Missouri Kid's time had finally run out. On May 8, 1905, he bade goodbye to his mother from his jail cell and then was led to the gallows. A crowd of over two hundred people, limited in size only because the small jail yard could not accommodate more, gathered to witness the spectacle and included many female admirers. Because Rudolph was hanged using a short rope, the same one that had been used to hang his partner, he writhed in agony for several minutes before dying of strangulation.

14

The Lynching Era in the Ozarks

From 1882 to 1940, about 4,700 lynchings, most concentrated during a thirty-year period from 1889 to 1918, occurred in the United States, and over 3,400 of the victims were black. The lynching era began with the end of Reconstruction. With Federal troops no longer present to ensure order, some Southern whites used force and intimidation to keep blacks "in their place." The border state of Missouri witnessed its share of lynchings, too.

The word "lynch" is derived from Charles Lynch, a Revolutionary War colonel and wealthy Virginia plantation owner who headed up a vigilante "court" after the war that meted out punishment to Tories without the benefit of a trial. In the beginning, "lynching" did not normally result in the death of the victim. Usually the person was simply beaten, but after 1850, lynchings took a brutal turn, as victims began to be burned at the stake, dismembered, or hanged. The term "lynching" has now come to mean the extra-legal killing of a person, especially by hanging, in the name of mob justice.

Even before 1882, lynchings were not altogether uncommon in the Ozarks. For example, the "Regulators," a vigilante group that operated in Greene County, Missouri shortly after the Civil War, shot and killed Green B. Phillips on May 23, 1866, near Cave Springs for supposedly aiding and abetting thieves in the area. Three days later, they hanged two men from a redbud tree near Walnut Grove for too vigorously protesting the first killing. Just a few days later, the "Honest Man's League," as they called themselves, rode onto the Springfield square, 200 strong, briefly took possession of the place, and then rode out toward Ozark. There they captured a fugitive from Greene County charged with theft and strung him up to a nearby tree.

One of the first extra-legal killings in the Ozarks during the "lynching era" that began in 1882 was also strictly an act of vigilantism that had nothing to do with race. In early April of 1885, Frank and Tubal Taylor of Taney County, Missouri, were arrested on felonious-assault charges and jailed at Forsyth after robbing and shooting a storeowner a few miles outside town. On the night of April 15, a mob of Bald Knobbers, a "Citizens Committee" that had recently formed in the area to combat rampant lawlessness, broke into the jail, took the two men a couple of miles northwest of town, and strung them up to a tree on Swan Creek.

One of the first lynchings with racial overtones in the region occurred on December 14, 1891, when an unidentified black man passing through Newton County, Arkansas, was hanged from the Pruitt Bridge north of Jasper for some alleged crime. According to local lore, the hanging was largely meant as a warning to other blacks that they were not welcome in the county.

Another early lynching occurred at Lamar, Missouri, on January 23, 1892. A few days before, a local woman and her six-year-old son had been bashed to death with a chair and poker. A little girl who had been left for dead regained consciousness and identified a black man named Robert Hepler as the murderer. He was arrested and supposedly admitted the heinous deed. He was taken to jail at Nevada to avoid mob law, but the feared mob, 200 strong, formed nonetheless on the evening of January 22 and took a train to Nevada. They wrested the victim from his cell, took him back to Lamar on another train, and hanged him on the courthouse square at 1:30 in the morning.

In March of 1892 in Taney County, an unruly mob broke into the Forsyth jail, shot and killed a deputy sheriff in the process, dragged a wife murderer named John Wesley Bright from his cell, and hanged him from a tree at a nearby cemetery. This action was the last gasp of vigilantism in Taney County. However, it had little connection to the Bald Knobber movement that preceded it and, like the lynching of the Taylors, had nothing to do with race.

On April 25, 1899, Galena, Kansas, witnessed the rare instance of an African-American being lynched by men of his own race. A man named Charles Williams, who had been arrested on suspicion of strangling his sweetheart to death, was killed by a mob of black men who broke into the jail at 2:30 in the morning. The mob, according to the *Joplin Daily Globe*, "invited Williams to be lynched" and shot him four times when he "showed fight."

One of the more sensational lynchings in the Ozarks occurred at Pierce City, Missouri (spelled Peirce City at the time) in August of 1901. A young woman named Gisela Wild was killed while walking home from church south of Pierce City on Sunday, August 18. Her brother, trailing her home, found her body beneath a railroad bridge, and someone reported seeing a black man, believed to be Joe Lark, sitting on the bridge not long before the murder. While search parties unsuccessfully hunted for Lark, two other suspects, Will Godley and Gene Carter, were arrested and locked in the city jail. On the evening of August 19, as the search parties returned to town, a mob of 1,200 men formed in the streets of Pierce City. Around nine o'clock, the frenzied horde seized Godley and Carter from the jail and, firing off random gunshots that broke out numerous windows and injured several bystanders, paraded their captives through the streets with ropes tied around their necks. They returned Carter to the jail when he supposedly implicated Lark in the murder, but Godley, who wouldn't talk and had served a prison term for rape, was hanged from the second-floor banister of the Hotel Lawrence and his body riddled with bullets.

The mob then set off toward the homes of the town's black population, intent on running all of the blacks out of town. They fired indiscriminately into the houses, and when someone from one of the homes returned fire, the mob fairly poured lead into the houses and set five of them ablaze. The next day, the cremated bodies of French Godley (Will's uncle) and Pete Hampton were found in the charred remains of one of the houses. The mob had, as the *Joplin Daily Globe* reported at the time, succeeded in making Pierce City "a white man's town."

According to Murray Bishoff, author of a historical novel about the Pierce City lynchings entitled *Cries of Thunder,* some of Pierce City's black population moved to Joplin, where they had trouble finding work. Also, the lawsuit of French Godley's widow against several Pierce City men involved in her husband's death was heard in Joplin in February 1903. So the atrocity in Pierce City may have been at least indirectly related to what happened in Joplin shortly after the lawsuit.

On April 14, 1903, Joplin police officer Theodore Leslie was killed in a shootout with several "tramp" black men, who had holed up in a railroad boxcar. The next day one of the suspects, Thomas Gilyard, was arrested and placed in the city jail. Shortly after 5:00 p.m., a gathering mob battered down the doors of the jail and took Gilyard from his cell over the protests of the jailers. Within minutes, a raucous mob of nearly five thousand people surged around the captive as city officials pled with the throng to let the law take its course and reminded them that it was not certain Gilyard was the guilty party. The bloodthirsty crowd hanged Gilyard, nonetheless, from a telephone pole at the corner of Second and Wall, and at least one shot was fired into his lifeless body. Many of the riotous mob then marched through the streets of Joplin swearing vengeance on all blacks and burning the homes of what the *Joplin Daily Globe* called the "respectable" black population. The mayor had to organize armed citizen patrols to regain control of the town.

Just as shocking as the atrocity at Pierce City and even more infamous are the lynchings in Springfield, Missouri on Saturday, April 14, 1906. The previous evening, a young married, white woman was cavorting with a man not her husband when two young black men reportedly accosted the couple, assaulted the woman, and robbed her escort. Horace Duncan and Fred Coker were arrested as suspects, and even though evidence at the time suggested they were innocent, they were held in the county jail. Around nine o'clock Saturday evening, a mob of men broke into the jail, dragged Duncan and Coker to the city square, and hanged them from the bandstand on the Gottfried Tower before the unseeing eyes of Lady Liberty atop the tower and the eager gaping of 5,000 spectators below. The mob then built a bonfire beneath the dangling corpses, cremating them.

The horde then surged back to the jail and pulled Will Allen, suspected of killing an elderly man at the edge of the Drury College campus, from his cell. They hauled their captive back to the square and placed a noose around his neck. After a mock trial, one of the mob flipped him somersault over the rail of the bandstand, breaking his neck with a snap when the noose tightened around it. The next morning, according to a *Kansas City Star* reporter, "the church bells rang as cheerily as if the night before had nothing to hide." Children on their way to Easter Sunday services rummaged through the smoldering rubble of the murderous pyre, scavenging buttons, pieces of clothing, and rope as souvenirs. Enterprising photographers took pictures for later resale, and other businessmen made souvenir medals, one of which commemorated the grisly event as an "Easter offering."

After the Springfield lynchings, many black residents of the city packed up and left the area, never to return. The exodus of blacks from the region after this and similar incidents has been called the "whitewashing" of the Ozarks, and even today the percentage of blacks in the region remains much smaller than it was during the late 1800s.

Spectators gather at the Gottfried Tower on the Springfield square on the morning after the 1906 lynchings. (Courtesy History Museum for Springfield-Greene County)

Grave of Fred Coker at Springfield's Hazelwood Cemetery.

Other lynchings in the Ozarks region and on its fringes occurred at Poplar Bluff, Missouri, in 1890; Nevada, Missouri, in 1893; Monett, Missouri, in 1894; Cherokee, Kansas, in 1894; Galena, Missouri, in 1898; Weir, Kansas, in 1899; Pittsburg, Kansas, where Montgomery Godley, cousin of the Pierce City victim, was lynched on Christmas Day 1902; and West Plains, Missouri, in 1914.

Strangely, Lamar, site of one of the Ozarks' early lynchings, was also the stage for its last, the hanging of a white man in the spring of 1919. In an odd twist, the victim was named Jay Lynch. He was strung up on the courthouse lawn on a tree that was planted by the sheriff he had murdered and that stood just a few feet away from where Robert Hepler had been lynched twenty-seven years earlier (see chapter 17).

The lynching era was an ugly chapter in American history, and the Ozarks, like much of the rest of the country, was stained by it. By retelling the stories, especially those with racial implications, we risk embroidering a mythology of hate for the bigots, but the stain is not truly cleansed simply by pretending it doesn't exist. Only by examining our history do we learn from it and move forward.

15

The Damnable Act of One Hell-Born Fiend

After twenty-year-old Joseph "Jodie" Hamilton killed Carney Parsons, his wife, and their three young kids north of Houston, Missouri, in October of 1906, the *Houston Herald* called the crime the "most brutal and dastardly murder ever committed" within the borders of Texas County. Some people, though, tried to find a justification for the unthinkable act. They said Jodie had been kicked in the head by a mule when he was seven years old and was "slightly demented." Some said the slightly built young man had been mistreated by his stern, Bible-toting father and by a stepmother he didn't get along with. Others attributed Jodie's heinous deed to the fact that the girlfriend whom he hoped to marry had recently rejected him. Jodie himself suggested that Parsons had cheated him in a business transaction and had been spreading lies about him.

Later, as Jodie's December date with the gallows approached, there were even those who tried to romanticize the murderer. He started issuing statements from his cell admonishing the young people of the community not to follow his wicked example but to keep to the straight and narrow path of the Lord, and cards and notes of sympathy, some containing poems or songs about Jodie, soon began arriving at the Houston jail. At his execution, he issued a final plea for those in attendance to learn from his example, and he elicited further pity when the rope came undone during the first attempt to hang him and he had to be hanged a second time.

Then, after his death, Jodie's story was told over and over in Texas County and passed down from generation to generation until he became almost a folk hero. But he was anything but a hero. While nearly all of the assertions that sought to diminish his responsibility for his crime contained a grain of truth, the harder truth was simply that he was guilty of what the *Herald* called "the damnable act of one hell-born fiend," and he had committed it for no good reason except a fit of temper that "all come on me at once."

Jodie grew up in Texas County, but after his mother died, his father remarried and moved the family to Kansas around 1902. Jodie struck out on his own when he was eighteen years old. After wandering around the country for over a year, he came back to Texas County in August of 1906 and found a job working for sharecropper Carney Parsons on C. H. Cantrell's farm, about ten or twelve miles north of Houston in the same neighborhood where he had grown up.

Around the tenth of October, the thirty-two-year-old Parsons prepared to return with his family to Miller County, where he had formerly lived, and he sold his crop to Hamilton for twenty-five dollars. On Friday morning, October 12, the two men got into an argument as Jodie was seeing the family off. Reports vary as to the exact nature of the disagreement. One report in the immediate wake of the tragedy said they argued over the amount Jodie had paid for the crop, but Jodie later said the dispute involved a saddle. An elaboration on this latter story says that Jodie had stolen the saddle (or had found it and made no attempt to locate its rightful owner), that Parsons knew the saddle didn't belong to Jodie, and that he used this knowledge to get Jodie to come down on the price he was asking for the saddle. What all reports agree on is that the dispute involved a business transaction and that Jodie became more and more upset as he reflected on the deal after Parsons and his family had departed in a mule-drawn wagon. Feeling that he had been cheated, Jodie struck out across country to catch up with the family. He overtook them around noon along the Success Road a short distance west of the Big Piney River.

Jodie confronted Parsons about the deal they had made, and the exchange quickly grew heated. According to Jodie's version of events, when Parsons got down from his wagon and pulled out a knife, Jodie raised the single-barrel shotgun he was carrying and shot him. Blood evidence at the scene, however, suggested that Parsons was probably shot while still seated in the wagon. At any rate, the shot didn't kill him, and both he and his twenty-three-year-old wife, Minnie, began trying to wrest the weapon away from Hamilton. Jodie got the gun back, though, and struck Parsons a finishing blow to the head with the barrel. He then struck Mrs. Parsons in the same manner, but it didn't kill her. So, he beat her repeatedly in the head with the gun barrel until she was dead. Next Hamilton slit the throats of the two older boys, six-year-old Jessie Parsons and his three-year-old brother, Frank. They didn't die immediately, so he finished them off by crushing their skulls with the gun barrel as well. Finally, after a moment's hesitation, he battered in the brains of one-year-old Edward Parsons to keep the infant's cries from attracting attention.

After the grisly murders, Hamilton drove the wagon loaded with the bodies off the road a ways and unharnessed the mules. Taking Parsons's money and mounting one of the mules, he started off leading the other mule but turned it loose when it refused to follow. He rode the first mule back to the Cantrell farm on the east side of the river and early that evening rode it to the house of a neighbor named William Thompson, where he visited with Mr. and Mrs. Thompson and their two daughters. Later he attended church at the Cantrell schoolhouse, and he escorted sixteen-year-old Laura Fowler home after the services. A popular legend holds that Mae Thompson, one of the Thompson daughters, was the sweetheart who had recently refused Jodie's marriage proposal and that he went to church with her the night after the killings. It may well be that Mae had recently spurned Hamilton, but if so, he wasted little time in courting another young woman. Jodie himself testified that he went to church alone and escorted the Fowler girl, whom he referred to as "my girl," home the night after the murders.

After leaving the Fowler home, Jodie borrowed a horse from neighbor Al Decker and took it and Parsons's mule back to the scene of his crime west of the river. He hitched the animals up to the wagon and started with the bodies back to the river, but the horse wouldn't pull. About daylight he borrowed a mule from another neighbor, Ed Bates, and harnessed it up. Resuming the trip to the river, he saw a farmer named Jim Ormsby out on his front porch and exchanged greetings with him as he passed, carrying his gruesome cargo. It was sunup by the time he reached the river. He threw the bodies into the water and then drove the wagon into the woods a little way.

After unhitching the animals, he took the borrowed mule back to Ed Bates, returned to where he had left the borrowed horse, and took it back across the river to Al Decker. Still riding Parsons's mule, he visited several places on Saturday, including the small village of Prescott.

Meanwhile, the bodies of his victims had been in the water only an hour or so when a party of men out on an early Saturday fishing trip discovered two of the children. They could not be identified, but a short time later a blood-spattered wagon that was recognized as belonging to Carney Parsons was found in the nearby woods.

On Saturday evening, Hamilton went to the Fowler place with the idea of accompanying his girl to church again that night. But when he got there, the family was talking about the bodies that had been discovered in the Big Piney River, and as Jodie later testified, he "couldn't stand to hear them talking about it." Making an excuse that he had to go to

Licking, he said he wouldn't be able to go to church after all and "got up and pulled out."

Instead of going to Licking, though, Hamilton set out for Houston by way of Antioch, still riding the mule he had taken from Carney Parsons. Arriving in Houston around eight o'clock Saturday night, he went to Bob Williams's livery barn and stabled the mule. He tried to hire a saddle horse to ride to Cabool, where he planned to catch a train, but he was outfitted with a horse and buggy instead.

By the time Hamilton arrived in Houston on Saturday night, suspicion had already been directed toward him by those living near the crime scene, but the people of Houston knew only that the bodies of the two Parsons boys had been discovered. After Jodie left for Cabool, though, Williams became suspicious of the young man's behavior and notified ex-sheriff J. W. Cantrell and Deputy Sheriff Upton. They went to the livery, where Cantrell recognized the mule as one that had belonged to Carney Parsons. Cantrell telephoned J. R. Simmons, who ran a general store on the road to Cabool, and asked him to try to detain Hamilton. When Hamilton stopped at the store shortly before 11:00 p.m., Simmons insisted that he come inside for just a minute, and Jodie finally agreed. Cantrell and Deputy Upton rode up soon afterward, burst into the store with their guns pointed at Hamilton, and told him he was under arrest. He didn't resist but, instead, broke down and made a full confession. The lawmen searched him and found thirty-two dollars, a pair of glasses, and a razor on his person that had belonged to Parsons. Hamilton was taken back to Houston and lodged in the county jail about two o'clock Sunday morning, October 14.

Acting on information provided by the prisoner, searchers discovered the bodies of Mr. and Mrs. Parsons and their remaining son shortly after daylight on Sunday morning. The bodies were briefly laid out along the riverbank, and many spectators came by to view them before they were taken to a nearby home, where a postmortem was held on Sunday

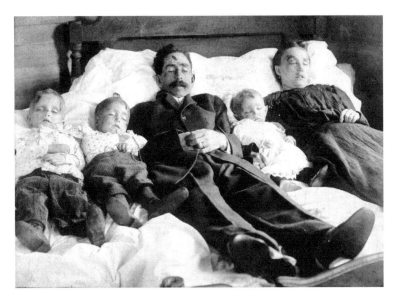

Bodies of the Parsons family, victims of Jodie Hamilton. (Courtesy Texas County Genealogical and Historical Society)

afternoon. Later, all five bodies were buried at the Cantrell cemetery.

Meanwhile, as word spread that Hamilton was being held at the county jail, an excited crowd started pouring into Houston from all parts of the county, especially the area where the murders were committed, and talk of a lynching intensified throughout the day on Sunday. Sometime on Sunday, Hamilton tried to kill himself by stabbing himself in the chest and neck with a darning needle he had somehow obtained.

On Sunday evening just after dark, Hamilton was whisked away to Springfield to avoid the feared vigilantism. At Cabool, while awaiting the train to Springfield, he again tried to kill himself, this time by repeatedly butting his head against a wall, and he ranted madly for most of the trip.

Learning of the prisoner's whereabouts, a throng of men from Houston came to Springfield on Monday, but by then Hamilton had been taken on to the Jasper County jail at Carthage. Unable to determine the prisoner's current location, the disappointed mob went back to Houston, and by the time Hamilton was brought back to Houston on October 22 for his preliminary hearing, the clamor for vigilante justice had subsided. The only witness at the October 24 hearing was ex-sheriff Cantrell, to whom Hamilton had confessed, and the prisoner was promptly returned to jail to await trial.

At his trial in Texas County Circuit Court on November 12, exactly one month after his heinous crime, Jodie made another full confession. Although "not brazen," according to the *Houston Herald*, "he seemed to have made up his mind to take the full consequences of his terrible deed." He said he didn't start out with the intention of killing Parsons but "it was just in my mind that he had either to straighten up with me and act up in the truth or else we would have trouble and that is what it come to." Hamilton suggested that he killed Mr. and Mrs. Parsons during his struggle with them, killed the two older boys so they couldn't identify him, and murdered the infant just to keep it quiet. At the end of the trial, the court passed sentence that Hamilton should hang on Friday, December 21, 1906.

Two weeks after his trial, Hamilton wrote a letter, published in the *Houston Herald*, admonishing his youthful readers always to tell the truth as he had done and always to heed the advice of their parents. Jodie defended his father and stepmother and said he was sorry for the pain he had brought them. Declaring his faith in Jesus Christ, he stated that he had asked for forgiveness of his terrible sin and that he expected it to be granted to him. "God be with you all," he said in closing, "till we meet again."

Within a week after his letter was published, Jodie started receiving sympathizing letters and messages. His father, J. B. H. Hamilton, arrived from Kansas and began trying, to no avail, to get Jodie's sentence commuted. Still, young Hamilton maintained a lighthearted and carefree attitude in the face of imminent death and was reportedly always "ready to play a joke at any time on his cell mates or the jailors."

On December 20, the day before Hamilton's execution date, the *Herald* published another letter from the condemned prisoner. Similar to but more spiritual in tone than the first one, it urged his readers to "step out on the Lord's side." After briefly recounting his life story, he said he was ready to meet his maker "with a good cheerful heart," and he closed the letter "hoping and praying that we may all meet in heaven." The same issue of the *Herald* also reprinted a mournful letter to Jodie from his stepmother that, no doubt, increased sympathy for the killer.

And most observers, even though nearly all of them felt that Hamilton richly deserved to die, could not help but be impressed by the seeming equanimity with which the young man faced his dire fate. According to the *Herald,* Jodie "passed his last days without apparent fear and was evidently possessed of a wonderful nerve that carried him through" the ordeal of being "face to face with the knowledge that death is a certainty and that his hours are numbered on earth."

On the evening before the execution, a song service was held at the jail, followed by a brief sermon by the Reverend W. I. Waggoner. Jodie listened attentively and then sang a song himself, after which he shook hands with those present and bid them goodbye.

The next morning he ate a hearty breakfast and showed "very little nervousness" as he was shaved and dressed for his date with the hangman. Hamilton was escorted from his cell at 10:42 a.m. and ascended the scaffold with "a steady step." The entire crowd on the courthouse lawn, estimated at three thousand people, joined in singing "Jesus, Lover of My Soul," although less than two hundred, who had tickets, had been allowed inside the stockade where the gallows stood.

Invited to address the audience, Jodie gave a brief statement that he didn't have any hard feelings toward the judge or the law officers, he had "owned up to it all like a

Scaffold scene at Jodie Hamilton's execution. (Courtesy Texas County Genealogical and Historical Society)

gentleman," and the officers were just doing their duty. He then sang a solo with the following refrain:

> Only a prayer, only a tear,
> Oh, if sister and mother were here,
> Only a song, 'twill comfort and cheer,
> Only a word from the Book so dear.

When Sheriff Aaron Wood, who was acting as executioner, asked whether that was all, Jodie launched into a rambling discourse that proved much longer than his first speech. Repeating much of what he had said in the two public letters that he had written while in jail, he admonished any young people present to take warning from his example and not to "follow the devil's way." Following a prayer by Reverend Waggoner, Jodie was asked one last time whether he had any final remarks. "So, dear kind friends," he said, "as my sentence has come, I hope to meet all of you friends standing around here today in a better world. Try to be faithful and meet God in peace, and hope to meet in a better world."

A black hood was placed over his head at 11:00 a.m. The young man started muttering, "Lord, have mercy on my poor sinning soul. Lord, have mercy on me and my soul." Sheriff Wood shook hands with him and bade him goodbye.

The trapdoor was sprung at 11:02, but when Jodie dropped through the floor, the noose jerked loose. He fell to the ground, still conscious but writhing in pain, as the spectators gaped in horror. A new knot was tied and slipped over his head, and he was carried back up the scaffold. At 11:04, the door was sprung again, and this time the knot held. The fall broke his neck, and he hung for fourteen minutes, with his toes barely touching the ground. Attending physicians then pronounced him dead, and his body was cut down.

The corpse was placed in a coffin, and many in the crowd filed by to view it. On Saturday morning, December 22, the body was taken to Allen Cemetery near Raymondville. Jodie was buried beside his mother, who had died when he was a young boy.

During the following week, poetic laments to Jodie's passing and even letters questioning the morality of capital punishment poured into the *Herald* office. One poem, called "Jodie Gone at Last," went like this:

> Jodie, thou art sweetly resting,
> No more sorrow here to bear;
> Thou art resting, sweetly resting,
> Where the shining angels are.

The songs, the poems, and the legend of Jodie Hamilton were repeated and orally passed down in Texas County. Even today, older natives of the county, even those who aren't particularly versed in local history, recognize the name of Jodie Hamilton and can tell you the rudiments of his story.

But who sang for the Parsons family?

16

As Mean as the Devil Would Let Him Be: The Last Hanging in Arkansas

When fifty-year-old Green B. Stephens of rural Delaware, Logan County, Arkansas, came in from the field on the late afternoon of Monday, March 10, 1913, and his twenty-year-old daughter Amanda wasn't home, he wasn't deeply worried at first. After all, Mandy wasn't a child. She was a free-spirited young woman who had gotten pregnant without the stamp of matrimony a couple of years earlier and had a baby who died at birth. She was old enough and independent enough to take care of herself.

Still, he was concerned and started looking around for clues as to where she might be. In her room, he found a note she had pinned to her pillow, saying she was going away to make her own living and asking him not to worry.

But worry is exactly what Green Stephens did, and he started asking around the neighborhood as to the whereabouts of his daughter. At the home of Mandy's cousin and friend, Ruby Smith, he learned that Mandy had been there that afternoon but hadn't stayed long and had mentioned that she might leave the area. On his way back home, Stephens stopped at the mailbox where he always picked up his mail. Inside was a letter addressed to Mandy. Retrieving it, he opened the envelope and found a note from a lover asking her to meet him at the "old place" and agreeing to get married if she still wanted to. Although the missive was unsigned, Stephens had to have known who sent it. Like everyone else around

Delaware, he knew his pretty daughter had been keeping company with twenty-two-year-old Arthur Tillman, a popular young man in the community who lived with his parents on a neighboring farm. The rumor around town was that the couple had been intimate, and whether or not Stephens had heard the gossip, he must surely have suspected as much himself. What had Mandy done—gone and gotten herself pregnant again?

Now, Stephens was more alarmed than ever, and he worried all night. The next day, upon a determined inquiry around Delaware, he learned that Mandy had been seen with Tillman on Monday morning and he knew she had been at the Smith house that afternoon, but no one had seen her since. If she was eloping with Tillman, though, why was he still hanging around?

Confronted, the young man claimed not to know where Mandy was. Stephens didn't believe him and threatened to file criminal charges against him. When Tillman left the community the next day, his departure seemed to confirm Stephens's suspicion that he wasn't telling the truth. That

(Left) Amanda Stephens. (Courtesy Logan County Museum)
(Right) Arthur Tillman. (Courtesy Logan County Museum)

evening, Wednesday, March 12, Mandy's father went before a local justice of the peace and swore out a complaint charging Arthur Tillman with the crime of seduction.

Tillman was located near Knoxville, a town several miles away in adjoining Johnson County, where the young man had gone to stay with his uncle. He was turned over to a constable from Logan County, but the officer, apparently viewing his assignment as a lark and the seduction charge as a joke, let the Tillman lad escape. How, the lawman must have reasoned, could you charge a man with seducing a gal who seemed to enjoy being seduced?

Tillman stayed in Johnson County for several days, visiting some other young ladies of his acquaintance, and then started back to Logan County on Sunday, March 16, taking a circuitous route. He avoided the main road through the community of Delaware, and as he approached his home about a mile southwest of town in the late afternoon, he stopped beside an old abandoned well on Ambrose Johnson's farm, adjoining his parents' property. Johnson and his wife, who had been away for an extended period but had returned the previous Tuesday, saw Tillman get down on his hands and knees and peer into the well before rising and continuing on toward his parents' house.

Aware of the disappearance of the Stephens girl, Johnson reported Arthur Tillman's suspicious behavior to some of his neighbors the next day and organized a search party. He and the other men went to the well and found the opening covered with sticks and planks held down by rocks that previously had served as a curbing for the well. Removing the cover of debris, they found many more rocks inside the well, and joined by Logan County deputies, they worked through the night and into early Tuesday morning hauling them out. At the bottom of the well lay the body of Amanda Stephens, with a bullet hole through her head. The corpse was partially submerged in water and held down by a heavy rock tied to her neck with telephone wire. A postmortem examination revealed that she was about four months pregnant at the time of her death. Evidence found at a cabin a few feet from the well suggested that the murder had occurred there.

Arthur Tillman was immediately suspected of the heinous murder, and a hastily formed coroner's jury concluded that he had committed the deed. News of the gruesome discovery on the Johnson farm "spread like wild fire" throughout the community, according to the nearby *Dardanelle Post Dispatch*, and "large posses of men began a determined search for Tillman."

By the time Mandy's body was dragged out of the well, though, Tillman had already fled the area again. After briefly visiting his parents, he spent Sunday night at the home of a nearby uncle. On Monday morning, on the advice of his father, as he later claimed, he caught a train to Memphis in an effort to avoid the seduction charge. From Memphis, he took a train back across the state of Arkansas to Fort Smith. A day or so later, word reached authorities in Logan and surrounding counties that a suspect fitting Tillman's description had been arrested in Van Buren, a few miles northeast of Fort Smith. Sheriff Ewell Love of Johnson County went to Van Buren to identify him, but the person wasn't Tillman. Continuing on to Fort Smith, however, Love met Tillman on the streets there and arrested him without incident. Tillman was then turned over to Sheriff Joel Cook of Logan County, who took him back to Paris and lodged him in the Logan County jail on March 20, two days after Mandy Stephens's body was pulled from the well.

Tillman's murder trial began in late August of 1913 in Logan County's southern district at Booneville, on a change of venue from Paris, and ended in a hung jury. The prosecution, though, must have been encouraged by the eleven-to-one vote in favor of conviction, because the defendant was retried two months later. Lacking eyewitnesses or other hard proof that Tillman had killed Mandy Stephens, the prosecution offered a mountain of circumstantial evidence tying the defendant to the crime. Not only had Ambrose Johnson seen him peering into the well where her body was found, but numerous other circumstances suggesting his guilt came to light.

On Sunday, March 9, the day before Mandy's disappearance, Tillman had gone to a physician in the Delaware area, stating that the young woman was pregnant as a result of his relations with her and asking for some sort of medicine or other remedy that would abort the unborn child. The doctor told Tillman he had no such medicine. The following morning, March 10, Tillman mailed the letter at the Delaware post office that Green Stephens read later that day, in which the young man agreed to marry Mandy and asked her to meet him at the "old place" so that they could "fix this up." Shortly after Tillman mailed the letter, Mandy was seen passing the post office along a road that ran toward her home, which was located about a mile northeast of town on the Yell County line. Tillman caught up with her, and the two were observed heading toward a pine thicket that they often used as a trysting spot. Less than an hour later, Tillman emerged from "the pines," as the spot was commonly called, and came back at a trot toward the post office. He tried to retrieve the letter he had mailed but was told it had already been posted. Late that afternoon, around sundown, Tillman was seen near a store about a half-mile north of his father's farm at approximately the same time that some telephone wire in the vicinity went missing, and the stolen line exactly matched the wire that was used to tie the rock to Mandy's body. The prosecution introduced a witness who said Tillman was engaged to another young woman and had no intention of marrying Mandy Stephens. Other witnesses for the state testified that the Tillman family had owned a .22-caliber rifle, the same caliber with which Mandy was shot, and that Arthur's father, John F. Tillman, had given it away shortly after Mandy's death.

Arthur Tillman freely confessed that he had been having frequent sexual intercourse with Mandy Stephens for several months prior to her death and that he had written the letter that was mailed to her on March 10. However, from the time of his arrest, he consistently denied having committed the bloody deed of which he was accused, and he offered a ready explanation for most of the incriminating circumstances. He said the letter was in reply to one he had received from Mandy the day before demanding that he should marry her. According to Tillman's story, though, Mandy had later agreed during the couple's Monday-morning tryst to drop her demand and leave town if Tillman and another man, Earl Bolden, who might be the father of her unborn child, would pay her way. Tillman said he gave her eight dollars, all the money he had, and when she turned up missing, he assumed she had left town as agreed. He said he looked into the well where Mandy's body was later found because he noticed it had been disturbed and thought that some of his father's livestock might have fallen into it. Tillman, who was still in school at the time of Mandy's death, claimed the reason he was in the vicinity of the store near where the telephone wire was stolen on the evening in question was that he had walked there to buy school supplies but had gone back home when he found the store closed. Except for this brief outing, he claimed he had been home all that afternoon and evening, and his family backed up the testimony. He said that he had fled the area only to avoid the seduction charge.

One of the primary strategies of the defense was to attack the reputation of the victim. According to Tillman's story, not only had Mandy been having sexual relations with Earl Bolden, a married kinsman of hers, during the same period that she was engaging in regular intercourse with Tillman, the two men had, at one time, taken turns going to bed with her at Bolden's house. In addition, the defense tried to introduce testimony that back in 1910, prior to her first pregnancy, Mandy had engaged in sexual relations not only with the defendant but with several other young men of the community, including Billy Fisher, a hired hand who worked on a farm near the Stephens place. The prosecution objected to this line of testimony and the court excluded it, ruling that the alleged 1910 encounters were too far removed from the current case. The prosecution also introduced Bolden as a rebuttal witness, and he claimed he had never had sex with Mandy Stephens, at his home or anywhere else.

Moreover, the prosecution called witnesses to rebut Tillman's ready explanations for his incriminating behavior on the day of Mandy's disappearance and later at the well. The keeper of the store at which Tillman supposedly meant to buy school supplies testified that he would have opened the store for any customer calling after closing time and that Tillman well knew his policy in this regard. Witnesses living between the store and the Tillman home testified that the defendant had taken an unaccustomed route in going to and from the store.

Seeking to impeach the testimony of the defendant's family, prosecutors called to the stand a neighborhood couple who claimed they had overheard Tillman's mother admit that her son left home with a rifle on the evening of the murder and that he did not return for several hours. In answer to Tillman's explanation for looking into the well, state witnesses testified that the Tillman livestock did not customarily range in the field near where the well was located and that the fence would have been sufficient to keep them out in any case. The defense countered this latter argument, claiming that a whole section of the fence had been burned, and considerable time was spent debating the question of whether or not the fence was intact.

In addition to trying to incriminate Earl Bolden as Mandy's killer, Tillman and his lawyers suggested that Green Stephens might have killed his own daughter. The defense tried to introduce testimony that Stephens had made a statement shortly before the girl's body was discovered predicting that his daughter would be found in a well south of a certain road with a bullet hole in her head and a rock tied to her neck. Although these were the exact conditions in which she was found, the court disallowed the testimony as hearsay and not indicative of guilt, even if Stephens made such a statement.

On November 1, 1913, Arthur Tillman was found guilty of first-degree murder and sentenced to hang. A few days after the verdict, as he was being transported to the state prison at Little Rock for safekeeping, he escaped by jumping from a moving train as it passed through Perry County. He was recaptured about ten hours later, hobbled by sprained ankles sustained during his leap for freedom.

Tillman's execution was originally set for March 10, 1914, the one-year anniversary of the crime of which he was convicted, but an appeal to the Arkansas Supreme Court postponed his date with destiny. After the high court upheld the verdict and the execution was rescheduled for July 15, 1914, Tillman turned to Gov. George Washington Hays, asking for clemency. The governor granted a commutation hearing, but after listening to arguments from both sides and deliberating for several days, he let the sentence stand. Tillman's family and friends continued to lobby on his behalf right up until the scheduled day of his execution, circulating petitions and pleading for leniency, and certain newspapers across the state wrote stories sympathetic to the convict. Letters of support began arriving at Tillman's prison cell, and the governor started receiving letters from the general public urging mercy. Still, he held to his decision.

A story that appeared in the *Arkansas Gazette* in late June suggesting that Arthur Tillman was a "good boy" and claiming that the Stephens family did not object to commutation of his sentence especially rankled Green Stephens. He and his oldest son, Sam, shot off a letter to the *Dardanelle Post Dispatch* stating adamantly that such a claim was "false and without foundation."

The letter continued, "All we wish to say about J. F. Tillman, the father of Arthur and the man who made the statement, is to refer those who may be interested in his reputation to the criminal dockets of the township and county in which he lives."

Stephens and his son concluded, "As to the statement

in the *Gazette* that Arthur Tillman is such a good boy, we respectfully refer anyone who wishes to know about him to the teachers to whom his education was entrusted; and his father has on various occasions been heard to say that Arthur was as mean as he could be, or as the devil would let him be."

As Tillman was being brought back to Paris on Monday, July 13, for his scheduled execution two days later, he made yet another dash for freedom. As the train slowed for a steep slope, the condemned man broke his fetters and bolted for the door. After opening it, though, he hesitated just long enough for one of the deputies who was guarding him to pull him back into the car. Tillman's last hope vanished later that day, after he was lodged in the Logan County jail, when the county attorney refused his request for a respite, a reprieve that the governor had agreed to grant if the prosecutor and judge would recommend it.

Tillman said his tearful goodbyes to his family on Monday afternoon and then spent most of the next day in the company of a local minister, who conducted religious services and led the prisoner in prayer and singing. During his final hours, Tillman reasserted his claim that Earl Bolden had committed the crime for which Tillman was getting ready to pay with his life.

The condemned man slept little on Tuesday night, and the next morning he was so overcome, some say by a drug that had been slipped to him, that he had to be virtually carried from his cell. A large group of curious onlookers gathered round as Tillman mounted the scaffold, but only about twenty-five were allowed inside the enclosure to witness the execution. The minister led the group in singing "Shall We Gather at the River," and Tillman joined in. Before the hood was placed over his head, he made a final statement still proclaiming his innocence. Shortly after 7:00 a.m. on July 15, 1914, Arthur Tillman dropped through the trapdoor to his death, becoming the last man legally hanged in the state of Arkansas. A newly installed electric chair at the state prison in Little Rock would soon become the mode of execution.

Arthur Tillman is led to the scaffold. (Courtesy Logan County Museum)

Tillman's friends and family adamantly claimed at the time of Mandy Stephens's death that he was not guilty of the crime, and the controversy surrounding the case has lingered into the modern era. In addition to Earl Bolden and Green Stephens, Tillman's father, John F. Tillman, has been named as a possible killer of Mandy Stephens. According to one story, he even confessed to the crime years later on his deathbed, but one wonders how a man could possibly let his own son die for something he himself had done. A magazine article appeared in the *Arkansas Times* in 1985 entitled "Who Murdered Amanda Stevens?" and a play based loosely on the case entitled *Marked Tree* premiered in Chicago in 1999. In the fall of 1913, however, twelve members of a Logan County jury were unanimously convinced that Arthur Tillman had killed Mandy Stephens in a lover's quarrel—convinced enough that they felt he should die for the crime.

17

The Greatest Tragedy That Ever Befell Pleasant Hill

A rash of crime along the Kansas City Southern Railroad line afflicted western Missouri in February of 1915, and Pleasant Hill, a junction point of the KCS and the Missouri Pacific, seemed especially hard hit. In the space of just a few days near the middle of the month, two railroad agents had been held up at the town and Oppenheimer's Department Store had been robbed, arousing the citizens to arms. City Marshal Joseph Adams, though, meant to do something about the spate of outlawry.

After Kansas City Southern special agent Henry Postlethwaite wired the marshal on Saturday, February 20, that two tramps suspected in a robbery at Richards, Missouri, the night before had escaped when he tried to arrest them at Hume, fifty miles to the south, and that the men were thought to be headed in the direction of Pleasant Hill, the fifty-eight-year-old Adams determined to keep a lookout for the culprits. Late in the afternoon, he and his night officer, thirty-nine-year-old Clarence Poindexter, spotted two strangers coming out of the Bastain Chappell Restaurant in Pleasant Hill, where they had eaten supper, and trailed them to the train depot. While the men were buying tickets for Independence, the lawmen strolled nonchalantly through the station, sizing up the dubious pair.

Back outside, Adams and Poindexter agreed that the two strangers were very likely the suspects in the Richards robbery, and they decided to make an arrest. While Poindexter stood guard at the depot, Adams hurried off to recruit another lawman to help with the task but quickly returned when he was unable to find the third officer. Since the Independence train was getting ready to leave, the lawmen had to act now. They reentered the depot accompanied by a private citizen named George Thomas, who had volunteered to help even though he was unarmed.

Approaching the suspects, who were seated while waiting to board the train, Marshal Adams drew his revolver and told them to put up their hands. One of the men, later identified as W. F. Williams, complained to Adams that he and his companion had been bothered all day and searched several times because they were apparently suspected of a robbery at Richards.

"Well," said Adams, "you won't object to being searched again."

"No, you can't search me!" snapped Williams as he sprang to his feet, going for his pistol and shoving it against Adams's stomach, even though the lawman had him covered.

Adams grabbed the barrel of Williams's pistol with his left hand and shoved it aside while opening fire with the revolver in his right hand. "A furious battle was on," as the editor of the *Pleasant Hill Times* phrased it a few days later. The unarmed Thomas ducked back outside and slammed the door shut as Adams engaged Williams and Poindexter exchanged lead with the second suspect. In all, nine shots were fired in less than ten seconds, three each by Adams and Poindexter, two by Williams, and one by the second suspect.

When the shooting died away, Thomas hurried back inside and found only Marshal Adams on his feet. His gun was pointed toward Williams, who had fallen back against his seat with a wound on his scalp and back and a bullet through his shoulder.

Poindexter lay still on the floor, and Thomas rushed over to him, crying, "Pointy, are you hurt?" Getting no response, he rolled the body over, and a great gush of blood flowed from a gaping wound near one ear. "He had died in the twinkling of an eye," according to the *Times* editor.

Photo of Marshal Joseph Adams that appeared in a local newspaper days after the shootout. (Courtesy Pleasant Hill Historical Society)

The second suspect, also shot through the brain, lay on the floor weltering about in a pool of blood and dying.

"Throw up your hands," Adams told Williams, "or I'll blow your head off."

Williams tried to oblige but could not raise his arms above his head. "You've got me," the wounded man said as Adams relieved him of his weapon and pulled him up into his seat.

Poindexter's body was taken to Parker and Hon Undertakers and later to the Presbyterian Church. A cursory examination of the second suspect suggested that nothing could be done to save him, and he was left on the depot floor until death overtook him about an hour later. He, too, was then taken to the local undertakers, where an identification card was found in his coat bearing the name of G. D. Ryan, but an area woman who viewed the body said he was a man she had known in St. Louis as Ed Miller. On the card, in the line for an address were the words "None of your damned business," and on the line for whom to notify in case of an accident was the word "Nobody."

Removed to a local doctor's office, Williams identified himself and said he was from Hot Springs, Arkansas, but he refused to tell who his mysterious partner was. After his wounds were dressed, Williams was taken to the local jail. The

Train station where shootout occurred, as it appears today.

story of the gun battle and the death of Poindexter, according to the *Times*, "spread through Pleasant Hill and out through the country like wildfire," and even though it was raining, "hundreds of angry men appeared on the downtown streets."

Yet the editor claimed, "There was no indication of mob spirit, the frenzied, excited, reckless mob spirit, as generally conceived." To the contrary, "a certain cool determination seemed to be in the air that the murderer should pay immediately the extreme penalty." As Constable Charles Talbot, the officer whom Marshal Adams had briefly looked for prior to confronting the two suspects, stood guard over Williams throughout Saturday evening, a constant stream of men visited the jail to peer through the bars of the cell at him.

When one of the men asked the prisoner whether he had a mother, Williams said he didn't but he had a wife and child in Hot Springs.

"Well, you ought to be with them," the visitor snarled. "You're in a damned poor place here."

When another man suggested to the prisoner that he was going to be lynched, Williams pled for his life. "For God's sake, men, don't hang me. I am human."

Despite their threats, the mob seemed to break up during the wee hours of the morning. Near 4:00 a.m., a steady rain was still coming down, and the streets were deserted. "To all appearances," according to the *Times*, "the angry men of the evening had gone home." Officer Talbot finally gave up his weary vigil and left to get some rest.

Talbot had scarcely gotten out of earshot of the jail, though, when "shadowy forms appeared as by magic, converging on the structure through the downpour." The band of determined men quickly sprung open the lock on the cell. Overpowering the prisoner, they bound his hands and feet, looped a rope around his neck, and gagged his mouth with a red bandana. They carried him to a nearby bell tower at the rear of the city hall building and tossed the other end of the rope over a board on the tower. Then they hoisted him up.

Bell tower where Williams was lynched. (Courtesy Pleasant Hill Historical Society)

Less than an hour later, Agent Postlethwaite, the man who had wired Marshal Adams to be on the lookout for the robbery suspects, arrived in Pleasant Hill, having learned of the previous day's shootout, and went straight to the jail to see the prisoner. Finding the cell empty, he phoned Officer Talbot, who hurried back to the jail. After a brief search in the predawn darkness, the two men discovered Williams's body swaying from the bell tower barely a foot off the ground. The red handkerchief used as a gag had slipped down around his neck, and the rain was beating down on his upturned face. Help was quickly summoned and the body cut down and taken to the undertaker.

Clarence Poindexter's funeral was held in Pleasant Hill on Tuesday afternoon, February 23, under the auspices of the local Odd Fellows lodge, of which the fallen officer was a member. The procession from the lodge to the M. E. Church South, where the service was held, was led by Marshal Adams and Officer Talbot. The minister who conducted the service had no words of censure for those involved in the lynching of Williams but instead seemed to suggest that, because of an anemic justice system, sometimes good men had to take the law into their own hands. The deceased lawman was buried in the city cemetery, and later the same day Ryan was interred in an unmarked grave at the same cemetery. That evening, Williams's body was shipped to Hot Springs, where money had been deposited by his family for his return.

A coroner's jury had concluded on Sunday that Williams came to his death "at the hands of parties unknown," and little effort was subsequently made to determine the identity of the men who carried out the vigilante hanging. Although Williams and Ryan proved not to be the Richards robbers, the general feeling around Pleasant Hill seemed to be that they must have been guilty of something or they wouldn't have resisted arrest. Most of the town's citizens, including the *Times* editor, shared the sentiment of the minister who preached Poindexter's funeral service. The editor reminded readers of the crime wave that had afflicted Pleasant Hill in recent weeks and said that the murder of Poindexter was the last straw. Although lamenting what he called "the greatest tragedy that ever befell Pleasant Hill," he said that the lynching had been done not so much out of vengeance but as "a warning to others that thugs, murderers and thieves have imposed enough on Pleasant Hill," and he suggested that the extra-legal hanging would serve "as a grim invitation to such gentry to give this town a wide berth."

18

Lamar's Lynching of Lynch: The Most Dangerous Man I Ever Saw

On the afternoon of March 2, 1919, W. Earl Gowdy, city marshal of Liberal, Missouri, and three other men arrested J. W. Lynch, Jr., and delivered him to the county jail at Lamar. There, Gowdy told Barton County sheriff John M. Harlow that Lynch was the "most dangerous man I ever saw." Sheriff Harlow laughed and thought it was a "great joke" that it took four men to bring in one petty burglar. As the *Lamar Democrat* editor, Arthur Aull, later observed, though, Marshal Gowdy proved to be "either some reader of a crook's general makeup, or else he made a wonderfully good guess."

Lynch had been arrested in August of 1918 for robbing boxcars in the St. Louis train yards but had skipped bond. He had committed the crime while serving, under the alias of George Owens, as a special detective for the Wabash Railroad, a job for which he was considered especially suited because of his "good nerve" and his marksmanship with a gun. Unbeknown even to Marshal Gowdy, though, the St. Louis burglary was only one in a long list of crimes for which Lynch was wanted, and the catalog of assumed names he had operated under was almost as lengthy.

Lynch, who was usually called "Jay," was born at Rich Hill, Missouri, around 1890, and neighbors there, after he became notorious, remembered that he had been a "bad boy" even as a child. The family later lived at Richards, Missouri; Kansas City; and Olathe, Kansas. Jay got married when he was only seventeen or eighteen years old, but his wife died after just six months. Around this same time, Lynch briefly tried his hand at farming but soon lost interest and struck out on his own.

In 1909, he was arrested in St. Louis for burglary and sentenced to the state reform school at Boonville. He promptly escaped and was arrested nine months later at Kansas City for stealing $60 worth of horseshoes. Sentenced to two years in the state penitentiary, he was paroled without serving any time. Lynch then got into a scrape in Oklahoma City in November of 1910 for car theft and another one in Kansas City in May of 1911 for stealing silks and women's clothing. The next year he pled guilty to robbing a post office and was fined $1,000 and sentenced to six months in jail. He escaped in October of 1912 but was recaptured in April of 1913. Let off with a suspended sentence, he lit out for Denver, where he was arrested for highway robbery in August of 1913. He was given a sentence of nine to fourteen years in the Colorado State Penitentiary, but he escaped three years later while serving as a prison trusty and promptly resumed his criminal career. In addition to being wanted for the prison escape in Colorado and robbing the boxcars in St. Louis, he was wanted for a burglary he committed in Buffalo, New York, in 1917. In between escapades, though, he found time to get remarried to a girl named Leola, whom he met in Ohio.

In the early 1910s, Lynch's unmarried sister, Stella, had moved to Barton County and settled at a farmhouse northeast of Verdella near the Vernon County line. She lived there off and on but also spent time in Kansas City with her and Jay's married sister, Pearl. Jay's parents—J. W., Sr., and Maude—stayed at the farm part of the time, too, when they weren't traveling around the country selling eyeglasses, or sometimes the old man would take off on his own and leave Maude there by herself. Occasionally Jay would drop in but rarely stayed long.

In the fall of 1918, he brought his pregnant young wife to the farm and deposited her there before heading back out. The baby was born in December, but Leola stayed on at the farm. To anyone who asked, she introduced herself as Mrs. George Owens, and Maude let it be known around Verdella that the young woman staying at her house was her nephew's wife. Then in February of 1919, the "nephew" showed back up.

Not everyone was fooled. Neighbor Dick Metcalf suspected the young man's real identity, and he knew Jay Lynch was wanted in St. Louis. When he relayed his suspicions to Sheriff Harlow, the lawman told him that he had already been out to the Lynch place. Jay had recognized him and took off running, but Harlow didn't want to shoot him. So, he offered to deputize Metcalf and let him organize a posse and make the arrest himself.

Metcalf took him up on the suggestion and recruited his brother Arthur Metcalf, Marshal Gowdy, and Deputy Sheriff Jim Pinkerton to compose the posse. When they got to the Lynch farm that Sunday afternoon, they found Jay in the barn cleaning out troughs. Dick Metcalf drew his pistol and told Lynch he was under arrest. "Well, you've got me," Lynch said with resignation as he raised his hands.

He then asked to be allowed to go to the house to get some clothes, and the request was granted. Three of the deputies accompanied him inside and watched as he rummaged around in several drawers. The lawmen suspected he was looking for a weapon, but they kept such a close guard on the prisoner that he had no chance to attempt an escape.

Now, they had their man safely back at Lamar and were turning him over to Sheriff Harlow. At the jail door, Lynch turned back to Dick Metcalf with an angry threat. "Damn you," he swore, "I'll get you as soon as I'm out of this, if it's twenty years."

To Sheriff Harlow, though, the new prisoner didn't seem any more menacing than the other petty crooks he was used to dealing with. On Monday morning, Lynch's wife and mother showed up at the jail, asked to visit the prisoner, and were granted permission to converse with him through the bars of the cell. After awhile, Maude said she had to go back home and get a letter for her son, and she asked that Leola, or Mrs. Owens as she continued to call herself, be allowed to go inside the cell with her baby to visit Jay while Mrs. Lynch was gone. After some hesitation, the sheriff's wife consented to the request. In midafternoon, Maude returned and was again allowed to talk to her son "a good long time" through the bars of the cell. Late in the afternoon, Maude asked that Leola and the baby be let out of the cell so the three of them could depart.

Meanwhile, Sheriff Harlow was making preparations to escort the prisoner to St. Louis that evening on the 7:55 Missouri Pacific passenger train. After being served dinner inside his cell, Lynch asked permission to use the telephone in the hallway that connected the jail proper to the dining room so that he could call his wife, who was now back at the farm. The sheriff, who, according to the local newspaper, was "always kind and indulgent with prisoners," granted the request and stood in the doorway to the dining room as Lynch made the call.

As soon as Lynch hung up, he whipped out a pistol that he had concealed somewhere in his clothes and, pointing it at Harlow, told the sheriff to put up his hands.

"You put up your hands," Harlow retorted as he reached for his gun.

The sheriff had barely cleared leather when Lynch opened fire. Three or four bullets struck Harlow, including two in the chest. As he collapsed to the floor, he called out to his wife, who was nearby, "He's shot me, Mother. Goodbye and God bless you."

Sheriff Harlow also tried to warn his eighteen-year-old son, Dick, as he entered the front (or south) door of the jail about the time the shooting began, but Lynch fired a single shot at the lad from about ten feet away that struck him in the chest. "Damn you, I'll kill everyone of you!" Lynch is reported to have exclaimed as young Harlow fell to the floor. Sheriff Harlow died about ten minutes after the shooting, just as a doctor arrived on the scene, and his son died less than a week later.

After the shooting, Lynch raced out the back (or north) door of the jail and ran down alleys, cut across yards, and scaled fences until he disappeared at the edge of town in the gathering darkness. A large manhunt was organized that included bloodhounds brought in from Carthage and Springfield, but to no avail. Deputies under Dick Metcalf kept a close watch on the Lynch farmhouse all night, thinking Jay might show up there. When he didn't, his mother and wife were arrested early Tuesday morning as suspected accomplices in the murders and taken to jail at Lamar.

Meanwhile, Lynch spent almost a week skulking through woods and prairies, hiding out in barns, and going without food before finally making it to Oskaloosa, near the Kansas border, where he hopped a freight train to Kansas City. From there he caught another freight to St. Louis, where he stayed with an old woman who had befriended him before. She fed and nursed him until he had his strength back, and he was also able somehow to get hold of $1,000 while he was in St. Louis. After a couple of weeks, he went to the Springfield, Illinois, area, where he bought a used car and struck out for the West Coast. In Los Angeles, he made the acquaintance of a young man named Eddie Williams, who became Lynch's traveling companion. After wandering around the West Coast for several days, they sold Lynch's car and took a train to La Junta, Colorado, a town Lynch had passed through on his way west.

When the train pulled into the station at La Junta late in the morning of May 13, 1919, and Lynch disembarked to get something to eat, one of the first people he saw on the street was John Bradshaw. A hunting buddy he had known back in Olathe, Kansas, Bradshaw was now living in La Junta. Lynch walked on, hoping he hadn't been recognized, but no such luck. Bradshaw went looking for a law officer and soon located Undersheriff Kenny Wood and a deputy named Martinez, who were near the train station. Lynch had reboarded, and the train was getting ready to pull back out when Bradshaw and the two lawmen entered the car where Lynch and his traveling companion were seated. Bradshaw pointed the fugitive out to the officers, and Deputy Martinez kept Williams covered as Undersheriff Wood stuck a big pistol in Lynch's face and placed him under arrest. Lynch later boasted he never would have let himself be taken in such a manner if he had a gun on his person, but he and Williams had put their guns away in suitcases while they were traveling on the train.

In addition to weapons and a lot of ammunition, various burglary tools were found in the suitcases belonging to Lynch and Williams, and Williams, although he claimed not to know Lynch, was detained along with his traveling partner. Wanted posters that had been circulated throughout the country after Lynch's murder of Sheriff Harlow helped La Junta authorities confirm the identification made by Bradshaw, and arrangements were quickly made for the fugitive's return to Missouri.

Sheriff Harlow's successor, Will Sewell, left Barton County for Colorado on Wednesday evening, May 14. After initially balking at the extradition, Lynch agreed to return to Missouri if he wouldn't be taken to Lamar for trial. Sewell agreed and brought the prisoner to Butler, where he was lodged in the Bates County jail on May 19. Lynch later changed his mind and agreed to go to Lamar for trial if he would be allowed to see his wife for at least an hour.

Fearing mob action, authorities arranged for a hasty trial. They made plans to whisk Lynch in and out of Lamar as inconspicuously as possible, but when Sheriff Sewell and several deputies brought Lynch to town aboard a train in

the early afternoon of May 28, 1919, word of their coming
had preceded them. An angry crowd had gathered to greet
the prisoner, and he was taken quickly by automobile to the
courthouse. The swelling throng followed and, according
to Editor Aull, began pouring into the courtroom "like
a torrent, filling every corner, all of them standing up,
craning their necks for the first glimpse of Lynch." By the
time the prisoner, who had been held briefly at the sheriff's
office while final arrangements for the trial were made, was
marched in, the chamber was completely packed.

Lynch was taken into Judge B. G. Thurman's private office
to await the judge's arrival. When Thurman showed up a few
minutes later, he announced the opening of court, and Lynch
was ushered back into the courtroom. After a reading of the
charges, Thurman told the defendant to stand and answer
the charges, and he stood up and pled guilty to the murder
of Sheriff Harlow and his son. Asked if he had anything to say
before sentence was pronounced, Lynch shook his head and
said, "No."

Judge Thurman then sentenced him to life imprisonment
at the state penitentiary. This was the severest sentence
allowed, because Missouri legislators had passed a law in
1917 abolishing capital punishment.

Sensing the angry mood of the court spectators and their
frustration with the new law, Judge Thurman spoke directly
to the crowd, telling them that, if they tried to take the law
into their own hands, they would regret it. As Lynch was
being led back to the judge's office, though, a man in the
rear of the courtroom yelled, "String him up!"

Sheriff Sewell and his deputies quickly restored order,
but within minutes after the proceedings concluded, a
knot of men gathered ominously on the lawn outside the
courthouse. One of them was carrying a suitcase "as to the
contents of which there was no mystery," and when a second
man pointed to a small elm tree near the courthouse steps,
the others nodded. One of the men hollered, "Let's go get

him!" According to Editor Aull, "It was evident . . . that the time was not yet arrived when they would actually 'get' him, but it was equally evident that it was not far distant."

Throughout the afternoon, the throng on the courthouse grounds continued to grow until it approached a thousand people. "The mob spirit kindled and flared," said Editor Aull, "and the prisoner remained up there in the death trap, like a rat, waiting to be thrown to a pack of terriers."

Finally, about 3:40 in the afternoon, a bloodcurdling yell went up. People rushed from their stores to the courthouse grounds, and the throng already gathered there pressed in around the steps leading to the building. About fifty men hurried inside and up the stairs to the judge's office, where the shackled prisoner was being allowed a promised visit with his wife and baby. Leola fainted as the men burst in, overpowered the sheriff and his deputies, and slipped a rope around her husband's neck. The mob dragged Lynch out of the courthouse and down the steps. He was reportedly already dead by the time they got him to the elm, which, ironically, Sheriff Harlow had planted about twenty years earlier during his first stint as sheriff of Barton County. Lynch's body lay motionless on the ground as the rope was looped over a branch of the tree. As several hands took hold of the rope and pulled him up, an old man in the crowd piped up that the same thing ought to be done to some of the legislators who voted to abolish capital punishment. Then the rope was tied and the corpse left dangling in the air. "So ended the life of a desperado, and a murderer," observed Mr. Aull.

Sentiment against Lynch's mother and his sister Stella, who had angered many locals with her denunciation of Sheriff Sewell and prosecutor H. W. Timmonds, also ran high, and some in the crowd clamored to lynch them, too. So they were taken for safekeeping to the jail at Nevada, where they spent the night. (Maude Lynch was eventually tried and acquitted for complicity in the murder of Sheriff Harlow.)

After stringing Lynch up, the mob gave orders that his

body be left alone. The county coroner finally cut it down about 5:45 p.m. by order of Sheriff Sewell. It was taken the next day to Joplin and buried after a small ceremony in the Forest Park Cemetery.

Missouri governor Frederick Gardner demanded an investigation into the lynching, and newspapers throughout the state editorialized against it, although a few, particularly in the rural areas, sympathized with the actions of the mob. Despite the governor's call for action and the bad press, very little was ever done to try to punish the mob. Prosecutor

Death certificate of Jay Lynch, noting his mode of death as hanging by a mob.

Timmonds appointed a grand jury, but no one would testify against those involved. Timmonds said that some of his best friends had told him "they would rot in jail before they divulged the name of any one in the mob." Perhaps Editor Aull best captured the mood of the citizens of Lamar when he suggested that, if any of the offenders were put on trial, they would come out of it not convicted "but something closely akin . . . to popular heroes."

Six weeks after the lynching in Lamar and largely in response to it, the Missouri legislature passed a bill rescinding the 1917 act abolishing capital punishment, and Governor Gardner promptly signed it into law.

19

Bonnie and Clyde Ride Again

Bonnie and Clyde's shootout with police in Joplin, Missouri on April 13, 1933, which was the subject of a chapter in *Ozarks Gunfights and Other Notorious Incidents*, is probably their most infamous exploit in this region, but the gang also made other incursions into the area, both before and after that event.

The notorious duo's first foray into the Ozarks came in late November of 1932, shortly after Clyde had formed his own gang. Bonnie and Clyde, accompanied by new recruits Hollis Hale and Frank Hardy, drove up from Texas and checked into a motor lodge at Carthage, Missouri. Running low on money, Clyde sent Bonnie to nearby Oronogo on November 29 to scout out the Farmers and Miners Bank there. The next morning, the gang stole a Chevrolet sedan from a home in Carthage, and the three men drove it into Oronogo armed to the teeth, while Bonnie waited just outside town in the gang's powerful V-8 Ford.

Hale stayed outside the bank in the Chevy while Barrow and Hardy entered the building. Waving a submachine gun threateningly, Clyde ordered the cashier, sixty-year-old R. A. Norton, and his lone customer, A. A. Farrar, to put up their hands. Farrar quickly complied, but Norton ducked behind his teller's cage and opened fire with a .38-caliber automatic pistol. Clyde laid down a stream of gunfire that splintered the wood and shattered the glass of the teller's cage but failed to penetrate the steel that lined the bottom part where Norton was hunkered down. Meanwhile, Farrar was hollering at the cashier to quit shooting or else he'd get both of them killed. Norton stopped firing and gave himself up, but only because his gun jammed.

Smashing a glass partition, the robbers stepped behind the cage, and Clyde approached Norton threateningly. "I ought to pump you full of lead," he snarled.

Outside, though, Hale began honking his horn impatiently. Hardy advised that they should leave the teller alone, just get the money, and get out. With Clyde covering the hostages, Hardy scooped up a small pile of cash beside the teller's cage, cutting his hand on the broken glass in the process. In their haste to escape, the bandits ignored a vault that contained much more money, and they hurried toward the door carrying barely over a hundred dollars. Outside, a posse of citizens, alerted to what was going on, had taken up arms and converged on the bank, and the two robbers emerged from the building with their guns blazing.

Oronogo bank building that Bonnie and Clyde robbed in 1932, as it appears today.

They reached the Chevy safely, but the bandits had to run a gauntlet of lead as about a dozen local citizens opened fire on the escaping vehicle. The robbers returned fire. According to a *Joplin Globe* report the next day, "Several townspeople narrowly missed being killed or wounded." The gang reunited with Bonnie about a mile and a quarter west of town, where they ditched the Chevy and made their getaway in the V-8 Ford.

A gaggle of police officers from surrounding towns arrived in Oronogo later in the day. After an initial investigation, the lawmen "expressed belief the bandits did not live in this vicinity." Their identity, though, was not discovered until over six months later when Hale confessed to his role in the crime.

On January 12, 1933, a month and a half after the Oronogo caper, the Bank of Ash Grove was robbed. Some writers have suggested that it was the work of the Barrow gang, but there is scant proof of this. What is known for sure is that Bonnie and Clyde were in the Greene County area later the same month.

At about six o'clock on the evening of January 26, Springfield motorcycle policeman Thomas A. Persell was patrolling near the intersection of St. Louis Street and Kimbrough Avenue when he noticed two young men and a girl in a Ford V-8 coach with an Oklahoma license plate circling the Shrine Mosque as though they were looking for a car to steal or burglarize. Persell followed the suspicious vehicle north across the Benton Avenue viaduct, pulled up beside it, and told the driver to stop. The driver, whom Persell would later learn was Clyde Barrow, turned east onto Pine Street (now Tampa) at the end of the viaduct before halting.

When Persell again pulled up beside the Ford and stopped, Clyde stepped out carrying a sawed-off automatic shotgun. He ordered the policeman to put up his hands and get in the car. Clyde jerked Persell's pistol from his holster and tossed it to his sidekick, W. D. Jones, as the officer slid into the front seat beside Jones. The girl, who would prove to be Bonnie Parker, had climbed into the backseat and was holding a .45 army automatic pistol.

Clyde, who appeared unacquainted with the streets of Springfield, told Persell he would have to guide him and his companions out of town. The gang drove to Glenstone and then started east on Highway 66 before Clyde asked if there was a back road they could take to the Joplin area. Persell said there was, so they turned back. Stopping along the road, they ordered Persell into the backseat and covered him with a blanket before returning to Glenstone. There they pulled into a service station to get gas, with Bonnie holding her pistol on the captive while the tank was filled.

Shortly after leaving the filling station, the gang uncovered Persell and ordered him back to the front seat. As he was climbing over the back rest, he saw what he called "a veritable arsenal" of weapons on the floorboard, including two rifles, two automatic shotguns, a Thompson submachine gun, and a number of pistols. He also noticed what appeared to be several bags of money in the car.

The pell-mell journey continued north on Highway 65 to Crystal Cave, where the gang took the Pleasant Hope road, and Clyde "batted along on that rough, winding road about fifty miles an hour." West of Pleasant Hope, the desperadoes briefly picked up Highway 13 and then took the muddy back roads through Morrisville and Greenfield, still doing almost fifty miles an hour. When they neared Golden City, they put Persell in the backseat under the blanket again while they refueled at a service station.

At first, Clyde was the only member of the gang to talk. He often asked Bonnie, whom he called "Hon" or "Babe," to check their whereabouts on a roadmap. Jones, whom Persell considered "a silent sort of chap," addressed Bonnie as "Sis," and she called him "Bud." All three gang members swore almost every time they spoke, and although Clyde didn't smoke, Bonnie "simply ate fags."

Bonnie and Clyde strike a playful pose. (Courtesy of Jasper County Records Center)

The gang continued west from Golden City, and when they came out on Highway 71 between Lamar and Jasper, they seemed to be back in familiar territory. Keeping to the back roads, they went to Carthage, where, according to Persell, they drove around awhile looking for a car to steal. Unable to find one to suit him, Clyde asked his "Hon" whether she thought there were any cars they could get at Webb City. When Bonnie replied in the affirmative, the gang drove to Webb City, where Jones got out twice to scout around but returned each time empty handed. The desperadoes then struck out for Oronogo and seemed to know exactly where they were going. When they reached Oronogo, they started laughing and talking about the gun battle they'd had in the town. Persell asked them about it, and one of them (presumably Clyde) explained that "some monkey in the bank took a shot at us." (At one point during his captivity, Persell also overheard Clyde mention Ash Grove, which seems to be the main evidence used to support the theory that the Barrow gang was responsible for holding up the bank there two weeks before Persell's kidnapping.)

From Oronogo, the gang drove to Joplin and cruised around in the Roanoke neighborhood in the north part of town, trying to find a car to steal. They finally gave up when Bonnie saw someone watching them from a window and suggested that they take off before the police came. They went back to Oronogo, where they stole a battery for the Ford they were driving and then drove a few miles outside town before stopping to install it. Persell tried to read the car's license plate while he was helping with the installation, but the tags were so muddy he could only make out a partial number.

Afterward, the gang drove around some more, passing through Stone's Corner north of Joplin shortly after midnight. They stopped about two miles west of the intersection. They told Persell that they were going to let him out and he could walk back to the corner, where there was a telephone.

Alighting from the vehicle, the gutsy Persell asked if he could have his pistol back, but Clyde refused, saying, "You're lucky as it is."

The Barrow gang then roared off toward Carl Junction, leaving Persell to trudge back to Stone's Corner, where he called the Joplin police. He was picked up shortly before two o'clock in the morning and taken into town, thus ending his eight-hour ordeal. Later the same day, Springfield police, accompanied by Persell's wife, arrived to take him back to Springfield.

About a month and half after the Persell kidnapping, a general store in Baxter Springs, Kansas, just across the state line from Joplin, was robbed on March 11 and again on March 18. Legend has it that Bonnie and Clyde were the perpetrators, but little solid evidence to confirm the lore seems to exist. What is known for sure is that the infamous showdown in Joplin occurred on April 13, 1933, less than a month after the second Baxter Springs robbery.

After the Joplin shootout, the Barrow gang fled to Texas, where Bonnie sustained serious burns and other injuries in an automobile accident in mid-June of 1933. The gang then retreated to northwest Arkansas and checked into a double cabin at a tourist camp in Fort Smith, where they planned to hole up until Bonnie recuperated. While Clyde was busy nursing Bonnie back to health, W. D. Jones and Clyde's brother, Buck, who had joined the gang prior to the Joplin shootout, began staging a series of holdups in surrounding towns to finance Bonnie's treatment and to pay other bills.

On June 23, they robbed Brown's Grocery in Fayetteville and were on their way back to Fort Smith when they rounded a bend near Alma at high speed and rear-ended a slow-moving vehicle in front of them. The irate driver got out of his vehicle and picked up a big rock in each hand. But he quickly discarded them and fled in terror when he found himself staring into the barrel of Buck's 16-gauge shotgun and Jones's .41-caliber pistol.

As the driver was making his dash for safety, Alma City Marshal H. D. Humphrey and Deputy A. M. Salyer, who were cruising the highway on the lookout for the grocery-store bandits, happened along and stopped to investigate. When Humphrey got out and approached the two disabled vehicles, Buck leveled his shotgun and knocked the lawman into a ditch with a load of buckshot. (Humphrey died a couple of days later.) Deputy Salyer returned fire and kept up a lively barrage in the direction of the wrecked cars as he retreated to the cover of a nearby farmhouse. Dodging the deputy's bullets, Buck got the lawmen's police car started and roared off toward Fayetteville but soon doubled back toward Fort Smith.

He and Jones later commandeered an automobile from a couple along the highway before rendezvousing with Clyde and the rest of the gang at the tourist camp. The next day, two men appeared at the door of a woman living near Winslow and beat her with a chain when she refused, even at the point of a gun, to give them the keys to her car. The assailants were thought at the time to have been Clyde and Buck Barrow, but this is disputed. What is known for sure is that the Barrow gang beat a trail to Texas and on to western Kansas promptly after Humphrey was killed so that they could lie low while Bonnie continued her convalescence.

The Barrow gang next ventured into the Ozarks when they showed up in Springfield on February 12, 1934, and stole an automobile from a residence on East Walnut Street. Shortly afterward, the stolen vehicle and a second bandit car were spotted roaring through Hurley about twenty-five miles southwest of Springfield. Clyde Barrow was driving one automobile, with Bonnie Parker, whom a Springfield newspaper called his "cigar-smoking sweetheart," at his side. The second car carried Raymond Hamilton and Henry Methvin, two ex-convicts whose escape from a Texas prison farm Clyde had recently engineered. Hamilton was an old sidekick of Clyde, while Methvin had recently joined the gang.

Stone County authorities were notified to be on the

lookout for the desperadoes, and Sheriff Seth Tuttle and several deputies pulled out of Galena on Highway 13 to try to intercept the gang. Just north of town, the bandits sped past in the opposite direction. The officers gave pursuit and soon came upon the car that had been stolen in Springfield abandoned at the side of the road about two miles east of Galena. Sheriff Tuttle took charge of the stolen car, while the deputies resumed the chase.

Meanwhile, the gangsters, having piled into Clyde's four-door Chevy sedan, raced toward Reeds Spring, where a roadblock set up by Constable Dale Davis awaited them at the underpass leading into town. The gang turned around when they saw the barricade. Davis jumped into his car and gave chase, but a barrage of lead from the fleeing vehicle caused him to hit the ditch. Briefly retracing their steps, the gang turned south on a side road, where area farmer Joe Gunn happened to be walking home. The desperadoes stopped and, explaining that they needed him as a guide, forced Gunn into the backseat. Continuing south, the gang came out on the farm-to-market road between Reeds Spring and Cape Fair (now Highway 76) and headed east.

In the meantime, the Stone County deputies had gone through Reeds Spring and doubled back west on the same farm-to-market road. When the officers saw the bandit car approaching, they stopped in the middle of the road and got out. The Barrow gang also halted in the road, and the three men stepped out with guns blazing, as the "auburn-haired bandit queen" reportedly cursed and squealed with delight. A heated exchange of lead ensued until the deputies ran out of ammunition, at which time the gangsters piled back into their car and drove by the lawmen, peppering the police vehicle with a final spray of gunfire as they passed.

Gunn then piloted the desperadoes to Berryville, Arkansas, where they took a second captive before turning both of them loose minutes later a few miles beyond Berryville. Gunn and his fellow hostage started hoofing it back toward Berryville.

Less than two months after the firefight in Stone County, Bonnie and Clyde, along with Henry Methvin, appeared in northeast Oklahoma, at the edge of the Ozarks, for another "episode of death," as a Joplin newspaper phrased it. On the morning of April 6, 1934, Police Chief Percy Boyd and Constable Cal Campbell of Commerce received a call from a citizen residing about a half-mile west of town that he had just passed a car mired in the mud near his home, that the occupants tried to get him to stop, and that he saw a cache of weapons in the vehicle as he passed. The lawmen immediately started toward the scene to investigate, with Boyd driving and Campbell standing outside on the running board with pistol in hand. The Barrow gang opened up with a submachine gun while the police car was still seventy-five feet away. Campbell returned fire with his revolver but was knocked from his perch with a fatal wound as Boyd brought the vehicle to a halt.

The police chief, who received only a minor injury, was held captive while the gang waylaid a passing truck driver and forced him to pull their car, a yellow V-8 Ford, from the mud. Letting the truck driver go on his way, the gang forced Boyd into the backseat of the Ford beside Methvin, and the bandit car roared away with Clyde at the wheel and Bonnie by his side. The gangsters headed west, skirted the southern edge of Chetopa, Kansas, and drove to Bartlett, Kansas. From there the gang made their way to Fort Scott and drove around aimlessly in that vicinity most of the afternoon and evening. As was the case with Tom Persell, Boyd was covered with a blanket and made to scrunch down anytime the gang stopped for gas or food. In the afternoon, when the Ford became mired again near Fort Scott, some high-school kids came along and tried to push it out, but Clyde quickly ordered them to go on their way. At one point during Boyd's captivity, Bonnie indignantly informed the police chief that she was not a cigar smoker, as the press made her out to be, explaining that the lie got started only because she had playfully posed with a cigar in her mouth on some film that was recovered from the scene of the Joplin shootout.

After the killing of Constable Campbell and the kidnapping of Boyd, a massive manhunt for the Barrow gang was undertaken throughout the tri-state area of northeast Oklahoma, southeast Kansas, and southwest Missouri; and numerous false sightings of the gang were reported. However, Bonnie and Clyde, after releasing Boyd unharmed south of Fort Scott in the wee hours of the morning on April 7, escaped the dragnet and made their way south. They were killed a month and a half later, on May 23, in a police ambush near Sailes, Louisiana, after Methvin betrayed them.

20

Wilbur Underhill: Lover's Lane Bandit to Tri-State Terror

Most residents of the Ozarks who have at least a passing interest in regional history know about Bonnie and Clyde's exploits throughout the area during the gangster era. Many are aware, too, of the Barker gang's ties to the region. But how many have even heard of Wilbur Underhill?

Growing up in Joplin, Missouri, Underhill got his start in crime as a teenage burglar in his hometown and quickly moved on to strong-arm robbery at a lover's lane on the outskirts of town. Later, between stints in prison, he pulled off a string of robberies throughout Missouri, Kansas, and Oklahoma and graduated to multiple murders along the way, earning the nickname "The Tri-State Terror." He was at the top of America's most-wanted list by 1933, and when he was gunned down in a shootout with law-enforcement officers in Shawnee, Oklahoma, later that year, he became the first criminal ever killed by officers of the fledgling agency that would become known as the FBI. Yet he remains relatively unknown in the annals of gangster history. Unlike the Barrow and Barker gangs, Wilbur Underhill was never romanticized in the press, and neither Warren Beatty nor any other leading man ever played him in the movies. Maybe the "mad dog of the underworld," as some have called him, was just too mean. But that, too, is little more than a caricature.

The real Wilbur Underhill was born in Newton County, Missouri, in 1901, and moved with his parents, Hank and

Almira, and his siblings to nearby Joplin in 1909. After the father died three years later, Wilbur's older brother Ernest started running with a gang, committing petty crimes, and Wilbur would often tag along. In 1913, Ernest killed a Joplin street vendor who refused to give up his cash, and he was sent to the Missouri State Penitentiary.

About this time, Wilbur was struck on the head by a case of empty glass bottles tossed from an upstairs window, and he was supposedly "never the same" afterward. Temperamental and given to violent outbursts, he quit school and moved to Neosho with a relative. His family had always spelled his given name *Wilber,* but he changed the spelling to *Wilbur,* because he thought it was more manly. Young Underhill returned to Joplin in the late 1910s and promptly got into trouble with the law. Caught red-handed burglarizing a posh Joplin residence in February of 1919, he got off easy with a three-year suspended sentence, reportedly because his attorney claimed the blow to his head a few years earlier had left him with brain damage.

Wilbur Underhill, though, as he would repeatedly prove, couldn't stay out of trouble. In the spring of 1920, someone started pulling off a series of strange nighttime robberies in a remote area at the southwest edge of Joplin called Tanyard Hollow. Sneaking up on young lovers parked in their Model Ts to kiss and caress, the lone bandit would present his pistol and announce, "This is a stickup." The crook would take whatever valuables the frightened youths happened to have and then flee on foot.

On the evening of June 4, patrol officer Ben Butterfield and three detectives of the Joplin police decided to lay a trap for the culprit by "posing as pleasure seekers," as the *Joplin Globe* phrased it. After driving to the out-of-the-way lover's lane, Butterfield and an unidentified young woman stayed in the front seat as decoys, while the three detectives hid in some nearby underbrush. Butterfield, feigning car trouble, soon got out and looked under the hood, and when a man carrying two revolvers approached threateningly, one of the detectives jumped up and ordered him to surrender. When he fired a shot instead, all three detectives opened up with a fusillade that included a load of buckshot. The startled intruder skedaddled into the woods but seemed to be hit.

A few days later, Underhill, suffering a wound to the leg, was arrested as a suspect. Identified by Butterfield, he was convicted of highway robbery in Newton County Court in October of 1920 and sentenced to two years in the state prison.

Released in December of 1921, the toughened, twenty-year-old ex-con moved across the state line from Joplin to the booming mining town of Picher in Ottawa County, Oklahoma. After briefly working in the mines, Underhill turned once again to crime, bootlegging liquor and burglarizing area businesses. When his gang split up, though, he went back home to Joplin, where, on the night of December 14, 1922, he pulled off what the *Joplin News Herald* called the "boldest holdup in months."

Walking into the Wilhoit Filling Station at Nineteenth and Main streets, Underhill covered attendant Dean Harvey with a .38-caliber revolver, pinched about twenty-five dollars from the till, mostly in coins, and then marched Harvey a couple of blocks through the streets at gunpoint before releasing him with a threat to kill him if he "squealed." Apparently taking the threat seriously, Harvey at first said he didn't get a good look at his assailant, but when Underhill was brought in for a lineup a couple of days later, Harvey picked him out as the man who had robbed him.

Held in the Jasper County jail at Carthage while awaiting trial, Underhill attempted to escape on January 8, 1923, by sawing through the bars on his cell window with hacksaw blades that authorities suspected his mother, Almira, and his younger brother, George, had sneaked in to him. The breakout was thwarted, though, and Almira and George were arrested as accomplices. (They were later released for lack of evidence.)

Wilbur pled guilty to robbery and was sent back to the state penitentiary in February of 1923. There he reunited with his brother Ernest, who was still serving a life sentence for murdering the street vendor. In June of 1925, Wilbur's oldest brother, Earl, was sent up the river for burglary, and less than a year later youngest brother George was convicted of larceny and joined the Underhill family reunion at Jeff City. In September of 1925, Wilbur was among a large group of prisoners who tried unsuccessfully to tunnel their way out of the state prison, but only the ringleaders were punished for the attempted breakout.

In November of 1926, Wilbur Underhill was released from prison and, after a brief visit to Joplin, once again went across the state line to the Picher mining fields, ostensibly to find work. Instead, he quickly jumped back into a life of crime. (Underhill claimed that the ill treatment he received from police and potential employers because of his status as an ex-con forced him back into crime.) Beginning around the first of December, he and a sidekick named Ike "Skeet" Akins pulled off a string of strong-arm robberies in the mining towns of the area, sticking up pedestrians on the streets. Then, on December 12, they and a third partner accosted a sixteen-year-old lad named Fred Smyth, who was walking down the street near a railroad crossing in Picher, and demanded his money. When the boy turned and fled, Underhill shot him with a .45-caliber revolver. Although seriously injured, Smyth survived and gave police a good description of his assailant.

During the next week or so, Underhill and Akins ranged into Kansas to rob the Roberts Grocery Store and the Milo Chew Drug Store in Baxter Springs and an oil company in Galena. They also knocked off a filling station north of Picher near the state line and were suspected of mugging a miner on the streets of that town and shooting him when he resisted.

The pair then went to Claremore and Tulsa before landing in Okmulgee, Oklahoma, on Christmas evening of 1926 to visit Akins's sister. Late that night they robbed a drugstore not far from the sister's house, and Akins killed an eighteen-year-old young man named George Fee in the process when the lad, thinking the heist was some sort of joke, refused to put up his hands.

The two desperadoes were discovered in Tulsa a few days later by Joe Anderson, a private detective hired by the Picher Mining Company to track down the perpetrators of the crimes that had occurred back in Ottawa County. Arrested and taken to Miami (Oklahoma), Underhill and Akins were soon recognized as the same pair who had killed the young man at the drugstore. They were transported to Okmulgee to face murder charges. While awaiting trial, though, they and two other inmates sawed through their cell bars at the Okmulgee County jail and made their escape in the early-morning hours of January 31, 1927. Underhill's doting mother was again suspected of supplying the hacksaw blades, but there was not enough evidence to bring charges against her. An intense nationwide manhunt for the fugitives ensued in the wake of the escape.

Instead of lying low, though, Underhill set out on another crime spree. On February 5, he and Akins kidnapped a taxicab driver at Pittsburg, Kansas, and forced him to drive them to Fort Scott before releasing him. On February 9, Akins was captured near Lamar, Missouri, and was killed trying to escape a few days later as he was being transported back to Okmulgee.

On the evening of February 13, Underhill held up a motion-picture theater in Picher and afterward calmly strolled into a drugstore a block away and ordered a soda. Emerging from the business, he was stopped by Constable George Fuller and a deputy named Earl O'Neal and told he was under arrest. The suspect didn't resist at first, but as O'Neal started to put handcuffs on him, Underhill jerked a gun from his belt and fired several rounds in quick succession, mortally wounding the deputy. Fuller and a night patrolman standing across the street opened fire on Underhill as he bolted away, but the fugitive made his escape by dodging between parked cars.

The next night, Underhill held up the Blue Mound Service Station north of Picher. As lawmen were arriving to investigate, he robbed another station a short distance away on the state line, where he was recognized by the owner as the same man who had held the place up only a few months earlier. The next day, posses of lawmen fanned out across southwest Missouri, southeast Kansas, and northeast Oklahoma, futilely scouring the region for any sign of the man whom a newspaper reporter had now dubbed the "tri-state terror."

On April 20, 1927, Underhill was wounded and captured at Panama, Oklahoma, and taken back to Okmulgee to face charges in the Fee murder. He was convicted in early June and sentenced to life imprisonment at the Oklahoma State Penitentiary at McAlester. After he and some other hardcore convicts attempted a breakout in August, Underhill was tossed into solitary confinement, and he soon earned a reputation, according to the assistant warden, as the "meanest man we have ever had at this institution."

After four years at "Big Mac," Underhill made his escape on July 14, 1931, while on a work detail. Once again, the hardened con wasted little time plunging back into the world of crime. In late July, a man thought to be Underhill robbed a filling station and then a drugstore in Wichita, and on August 1 he held up a theater in Coffeyville, Kansas. The next day he robbed a service station in Wichita and killed the owner, William Neely, in the process.

During the first week of August, Underhill managed visits to his mother in Kansas City (where she had moved from southwest Missouri) and his sister in Joplin. Back in Wichita on the night of August 13, with his nephew Frank Vance Underhill serving as his getaway driver, Wilbur knocked off a Texaco filling station. The next morning, police officer Merle Colver confronted Frank Underhill and his notorious kinsman while making routine rounds at the hotel where they were staying, and Wilbur shot him dead for his trouble.

Before they could get out of town, both Underhills were captured in Wichita later the same day, exactly one month after Wilbur's escape from the Oklahoma pen. Trying to protect his nephew from blame in the killing of Officer Colver, Wilbur pled guilty in September to first-degree murder and was sentenced to life imprisonment in the Kansas State Penitentiary at Lansing. (Frank was subsequently tried and found not guilty.)

At the state prison, Underhill spent much of his first year in solitary confinement or chained up like a beast because of his escape attempts and other incorrigible behavior. Released into the general prison population, he tried in vain to gain a clemency hearing before once again turning his thoughts to escape. He recruited several hardcore criminals to the scheme, including the infamous bank robber Harvey Bailey. On May 30, 1933, the group made their break by taking the warden and two guards hostage during a baseball game and escaping through one of the prison towers.

Mug shot of Wilbur Underhill. (Courtesy Kansas State Historical Society)

Once outside the walls, they stole a car and drove southwest into Douglas County, Kansas, before turning south toward Oklahoma. During the next few weeks, sightings of the gang were reported throughout the Midwest, and they were even implicated in the infamous Kansas City Massacre on June 17, 1933. Apparently, though, the so-called Underhill-Bailey gang spent most of their time in Oklahoma, where they pulled off two or three bank robberies before splitting apart in September of 1933.

After the breakup, Underhill reunited in the Cookson Hills with some of his old Oklahoma State Penitentiary pals. Over the next three months, he and his buddies pulled off numerous bank robberies and other crimes throughout Oklahoma and surrounding states, including stickups of the American National Bank of Baxter Springs, Kansas, on October 9, and the National Bank of Galena, Kansas, on October 30. The gang ranged as far afield as the People's National Bank of Stuttgart, Arkansas, on September 20 and the State National Bank of Frankfort, Kentucky, on November 23. Underhill was also implicated in several jobs that other members of his gang perpetrated, and he was blamed for several more that he had nothing to do with. Like many notorious criminals, he had become ubiquitous in the public mind, an ever-present bogeyman inspiring terror even from afar.

Acting on a tip from an unidentified informant, a large squad of federal and local officers finally cornered Underhill in a residence at Shawnee, Oklahoma, on December 30, 1933, and demanded his surrender. When he went for his gun instead, the cops showered the house with buckshot and automatic gunfire. They kept up the barrage as the wounded fugitive hobbled from the building, but he somehow made his escape through the storm of bullets. Underhill was found near death a few hours later, holed up in the rear of a used-furniture store sixteen blocks from the scene of the ambush. Suffering four .45-caliber gunshots and numerous buckshot

Church in Joplin where Underhill attended Sunday school as a child, as it appears today.

wounds, he was taken into custody and transported to a local hospital. He was moved to the Oklahoma State Penitentiary on January 6, 1934, where he died a few hours later.

Underhill's body was brought back to Joplin, and his funeral was held on January 10 at the Byers Avenue Methodist Church, where he had sometimes attended Sunday school as a child. Approximately 1,600 people packed the church for the service, and another 500 or more curious onlookers milled around outside the building. At the time, the gathering was reportedly the largest funeral ever held in Joplin. After the service, the body was transported to the town's Ozark Memorial Cemetery for burial.

21

What a Man Sows, That Shall He Also Reap: The Last Legal Hanging in Missouri

When traveling salesman Pearl Bozarth stopped for hitchhiker Roscoe "Red" Jackson along the highway south of Springfield, Missouri, on Wednesday, August 1, 1934, he didn't know he was picking up a murderer. Born and reared in the Howard's Ridge neighborhood of Ozark County, near the Arkansas line, the thirty-two-year-old Jackson had left home when he was about eighteen. Sometime later he had married Dona Ellison, also from Howard's Ridge, and they had moved to Oklahoma and had four kids together. Recently, though, the couple had separated, and Jackson had turned to a life of crime. A few days before Bozarth gave him a ride, he had killed a man in Oklahoma and, after a ten-year absence from his old home, was now "trying to get to his folks" in Ozark County.

Bozarth owned a poultry medicine company in Evansville, Indiana, and he traveled throughout the Midwest peddling his products. A friendly sort who often picked up hitchhikers and did them a good turn, he took Jackson to Branson and bought him a meal. After resuming the trip together, the pair stopped for the night in Forsyth at Shadow Rock Resort, which was run by Buck Reed, an acquaintance of Bozarth's.

The next morning, Bozarth, with his passenger sitting beside him, got a fill-up at the Simmons and Wolf Service Station near the southwest corner of the Forsyth square for a trip to Ava. The salesman flashed a wallet full of bills when he paid for the fuel. Bozarth and Jackson then pulled away from the station and headed east out of town.

Two days later, on Saturday, August 4, a farmer who happened to be traveling down a deserted country lane about seventeen miles northeast of Forsyth, near the small community of Brown Branch, came upon a dead body in a clump of bushes at the side of the road, about a hundred feet north of the main highway. The subsequent investigation "led to a surmise," according to the *Taney County Republican*, "so crammed with inhuman baseness and depravity that it is hard to believe but the facts are hard and stubborn." The man had been shot twice in the head, his maggot-infested corpse was decomposing from having lain in the hot sun, and his wallet was missing. The coroner took the remains to Forsyth, where the slain man was identified as Bozarth by Mr. Reed and the victim's son-in-law, who lived in Springfield. It was deduced that the murder had taken place on Thursday morning, as the farmer had heard shots in the same vicinity at that time. Suspicion immediately centered on the hitchhiker who had left Forsyth earlier that day with Bozarth. The traveling salesman had apparently been betrayed and killed by the man he befriended.

Near the outset of the investigation, a man living in Forsyth came forward and said that, when Bozarth passed through town, he recognized the salesman's companion as a member of a work crew he had once been a part of at Gainesville. Following up on this clue, law officers tentatively identified the alleged killer as Red Jackson and were soon on his trail in Oklahoma. Taney County sheriff Will Pumphrey and Prosecuting Attorney J. R. Gideon traveled to the Sooner State and arrested Jackson when he drove Bozarth's car into the town of Wekoka. The vehicle had been repainted and a trunk rack had been removed, but it still bore Bozarth's license plate. The fugitive was brought back to Missouri on August 8 and lodged briefly in the Taney County jail at Forsyth before being transferred to the Greene County jail at Springfield for safekeeping.

As Jackson's mid-October trial approached, he was moved again, this time to the jail at Ava. But he escaped from the Douglas County facility in early October when a fellow prisoner, who had just been discharged, slipped him a saw blade with which he cut the bars. He then lowered himself to the ground with knotted blankets and made his getaway.

He was recaptured in Howell County near the Ozark County line in late November. On the twenty-seventh, he appeared in circuit court at Forsyth before Judge Robert L. Gideon, who granted a defense request for a change of venue and moved the trial to Stone County.

Trial began at Galena on Monday, December 10, 1934. Most of the first day was taken up by selection of a jury, and no witnesses were called until about three o'clock. "The trial was rushed from this point," according to the *Stone County News Oracle*, "and about noon Tuesday the case went to the jury." The jurors had no difficulty finding Jackson guilty of first-degree murder, but after two hours of deliberation, they could not agree on a punishment, with nine favoring the death penalty and three voting for life imprisonment. According to law in case of a deadlocked jury, Judge Gideon assessed the punishment himself, sentencing Jackson to death by hanging, and the execution was set for February 18, 1935.

After his conviction, Jackson reportedly confessed, not only to killing Bozarth but also to the murder in Oklahoma a week earlier. At the Stone County jail on Tuesday afternoon following his trial, he asked for a minister. The Reverend R. L. Whittenberg went to the jail, and Jackson told him he wanted to be baptized. He was taken under heavy guard to the icy waters of the nearby James River, where Whittenberg performed the service. After his baptism, Jackson asked permission to address the fifty or so onlookers who had gathered for the occasion. "If your days were numbered like mine," he beseeched the crowd, "would you be ready to meet your God? I hope the life I've lived will save someone's soul." The editor of the *News Oracle,* however, took the condemned man's statement with a strong dose of skepticism, observing that "it would be hard for anyone to understand how the life he has lived could save anyone's soul."

Late Tuesday afternoon, Sheriff Pumphrey of Taney County and Sheriff Seth Tuttle of Stone County left Galena with the prisoner, headed for Jefferson City, where he was to be housed on "Death Row." General Rogers of Gainesville, attorney for the defense, took an appeal to the Missouri Supreme Court that delayed Jackson's date with death for over two years. The high court finally ruled on the case on March 11, 1937, upholding Jackson's death penalty, and his new execution date was set for April 16.

Stone County officials prepared to carry out the hanging, although citizens of the county were, according to the *News Oracle*, "decidedly against the execution of Jackson in Galena." State law said that an execution was supposed to be held in the county where the trial had taken place, but the people around Galena felt that Jackson's hanging should occur in Taney County, where the crime had been committed. They believed that the execution would only bring unwelcome publicity to their community and be "a blot on the county."

However, Sheriff I. H. Coin, who had succeeded Sheriff Tuttle since Jackson's trial, claimed it wouldn't bother him a bit to spring the trap on the convicted killer. "I had just as soon hang Jackson," he said, "as to hang a yellow dog." Early in the week of March 15, Coin escorted some prisoners to Jefferson City, where he hoped to get advice on building a scaffold and other details concerning the execution. Since only a limited number of people would be allowed to witness the hanging, Coin started issuing passes toward the end of March. In early April, he traveled to Kennett to witness a hanging and get "a few pointers," and back home in Galena he purchased the lumber for the scaffold. On April 8, though, just after Deputy Sheriff George Norris had begun work on erecting the scaffold, word reached Galena that Gov. Lloyd Stark had granted Jackson a reprieve until May 21 so that he could study the case further.

Citizens around Galena greeted the governor's action with joy and hoped that an execution in their county could yet be avoided altogether. A legal hanging had never taken place in Stone County, and the local citizens, according to the *News Oracle*, wanted "to keep it that way." A law to abolish hanging in favor of the gas chamber as the mode of capital punishment in Missouri and to move all executions to the state prison at Jefferson City was in the offing, and Stone County hoped that it could be passed before Jackson would have to be hanged.

But over the weekend of May 15, the governor telegraphed Sheriff Coin that he would grant no further reprieves and that the hanging would proceed as scheduled on May 21 at dawn. The sheriff and his deputy stepped up preparations for the execution, including putting the finishing touches on the sixteen-foot-high scaffold at the south side of the courthouse and the enclosure surrounding it.

On Thursday, May 20, Jackson was brought back to Galena from Jefferson City, where he had converted to Catholicism during his stay and had reportedly spent much of his time reading the Bible, praying, and even preaching to fellow inmates. His father, Andrew J. Jackson of Howard's Ridge, traveled to Galena the same day with the Reverend Sterl Watson of Pocahontas, Arkansas, who was an evangelist in the Church of Christ, and the two men were there waiting when Roscoe Jackson got to town. The father, who claimed to be a great-nephew of Pres. Andrew Jackson, said he had not seen his son for ten years. A devoutly religious man, he wanted his friend Reverend Watson to serve as Roscoe's spiritual adviser as the younger Jackson faced eternity, and he seemed upset when he learned that his son, instead, had arranged for Fr. Michael Ahern of Springfield to be present during his final hours. Andrew Jackson and Reverend Watson visited with the condemned man in his cell for about two and a half hours late Thursday afternoon, and Roscoe assured his father he was ready to meet his fate. "What a man sows," he said, "that shall he also reap, and I am prepared to reap my harvest in the morning." After the visit, rather than staying around to witness the execution, Mr. Jackson headed back to Howard's Ridge to make arrangements for his son's funeral and burial service.

Thursday evening, curious people began drifting into Galena from surrounding towns. The residents of Galena watched the gathering crowds for awhile and then most went home, but the visitors "caroused throughout the night with the merriment getting louder toward morning," according to the *Springfield Daily News*. "Drink flowed freely, several fights occurred, and mechanical music boxes played loudly and raucously the latest swing tunes" as "the visitors celebrated the doom of a man who also had killed."

As sunup approached on the morning of May 21, the burly Jackson refused an offer of food but asked instead for "a

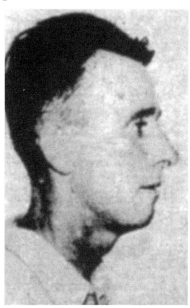

Newspaper photo of Red Jackson shortly before his execution.

good cigar." One of his last requests was to newspaper photographers who had been taking pictures of him in his cell, including one in which he was reading his Bible. He asked that they send some of the "good pictures" to his father in Howard's Ridge and his estranged wife in Pauls Valley, Oklahoma.

Shortly before 6:00 A.M., the entrance to the stockade surrounding the scaffold was opened, and "those who had passes surged into the enclosure," according to the *News Oracle*, "packing it like sardines."

In addition to the estimated four hundred spectators who crowded into the stockade, another one hundred or so stood outside, pressing in around the enclosure and trying to peek between the boards.

At approximately six o'clock, Sheriff Coin mounted the steps to the gallows, and Father Ahern, followed closely by Roscoe Jackson, appeared on a runway leading directly from the courthouse to a platform about halfway up the scaffold, with Father Ahern reading the rite of contrition and Jackson repeating the words after him. The condemned man climbed the final stairs to the scaffold with a firm stride. As the *Springfield Daily News* observed, "The convention-like spirit and the morbid and ghoulish delight with which many greeted the hanging failed in any way to break the iron composure of Jackson."

After completing the religious rite, he turned toward a window in the stockade and spoke to the crowd outside the enclosure. "Folks, not everybody realizes what it is to die," he said. "When a person dies accidentally, it isn't so hard, but when you die gradually, it is hard." Then he expanded on the topic of death, adding, "Everyone has to die, and I am going to die like a man." He touched briefly on the idea of forgiveness and then concluded by asking those who believed in prayer to pray for him. "I am leaving without any ingratitude in my heart toward anyone."

When Jackson turned back to face the crowd inside the stockade, he was placed in the center of the trapdoor. One lawman put the black hood over his head, another placed the noose around his neck, and others strapped his ankles and knees together. Jackson raised his manacled hands and said, "Well, be good, folks." Then Sheriff Coin pulled the lever that plunged him into eternity. He was pronounced dead ten minutes later, at 6:13.

The throng inside the stockade hushed only during the sacred rite, the subsequent statement by Jackson, and the execution itself. Then, as soon as the condemned man dropped through the trapdoor, they surged forward, eager "to satisfy their morbid greed to see if the eleven-foot fall had broken Jackson's neck—to see if he twitched and turned" and to watch the doctors "listen to his heart with stethoscopes as it came to a faltering stop," according to the Springfield newspaperman. "A few in the crowd were deeply affected by the sight of seeing a man killed . . . but the majority wanted to see all the details."

As soon as the body was removed from the stockade, the laughing and joking among the crowd resumed, and there was a mad scramble to get pieces of the hangman's rope as souvenirs. People continued milling around the square long after the execution, and children, who had been forbidden admission to the hanging, went inside the stockade, according to the *Joplin News Herald*, to "gaze in awe at the scaffold."

After the execution, Jackson's body was taken to Hilton and Manlove undertaking in Crane, where it was prepared for burial. The next morning, it was transferred to Ozark County for interment.

The execution of Roscoe Jackson stands as the only legal hanging ever in Stone County. It was also the last legal hanging in Missouri, because the law adopting the gas chamber as the means of execution in the state went into effect shortly afterward. Some historians, depending on their definition of the word "public," claim that Jackson's execution also marked the last public hanging in the United States.

22

Bobby Camden:
Robin Hood of the Ozarks

When Robert Camden was recaptured in July of 1951 near Centerville, Reynolds County, Missouri, after having escaped earlier in the year from the state penitentiary, where he was serving a life sentence for murder, newspaper reports referred to him variously as "the ridge-running Romeo," "the Robin Hood of the Ozarks," "the scourge of the Ozarks," "a one-man crime wave," and "Missouri's No. 1 fugitive." The first two nicknames were at least partly a product of romantic fancy, but he had duly earned the other three titles during a life of crime that stretched back over thirty years.

Bobby Camden was born in the eastern Dent County community of Boss on April 29, 1901. He was the son of George Benjamin Camden and Rosa Black and was reared mostly in neighboring Reynolds County by relatives.

Bobby was just seventeen when he first ran afoul of the law. In the fall of 1918, he and older cousins Enoch and Milton Barton teamed up to burglarize a post office and store in the Bartons' home community of Oates, in northern Reynolds County. The trio was apprehended and transferred to the Iron County jail in Ironton to await trial.

On the afternoon of November 11, 1918, while the Iron County sheriff was participating in a festivity celebrating the end of World War I, a trusty named Mike Kelly let the three young offenders out of their cell. The foursome ransacked the jailhouse, taking three revolvers, a gold watch, and some other articles from the premises, then made their escape and were seen about two miles west of town later in the day. That night, a store in Belleview, about ten miles northwest of Ironton, was broken into. The escapees were immediately suspected of the burglary, because the culprits stole some new clothes and left old ones matching the description of what they had been wearing at the time of their escape.

Late on the night of November 13, the fugitives stole four horses from farms in western Iron County with the intention, they later said, of riding south to get out of the area, but they decided to loot one last business before leaving. About midnight, the manager of a store in the small community of Doyle saw a suspicious light coming from his business and hastily organized a posse to investigate. The four jail breakers were caught in the act of burglarizing the store and ordered to surrender. The Bartons complied, but Camden and Kelly made a run for the door and escaped into the darkness amid a hail of bullets fired at them. The Bartons were taken back to Ironton on November 14. The next day, Camden surrendered in Bixby, another small community in western Ironton County, and he, too, was taken back to the county jail. Kelly was recaptured on the fifteenth and returned to the calaboose.

On December 9, Camden, the Bartons, and Kelly pled guilty to burglarizing the store in Doyle. The diminutive Camden was sent to the state reformatory in Boonville, where he was listed on the commitment register as five feet six inches tall and 120 pounds and was described as having brown hair and blue eyes. His term was not set to expire until December of 1921, but he was pardoned and discharged in March of 1920.

Less than two years later, though, Camden once again butted heads with the law, this time in Oregon County. On the night of December 26, 1921, he and a black man named William Moore held up Fred and Harry Warren at Thayer. Moore was arrested shortly afterward and pled guilty to the crime but identified his accomplice only as a young white man from West Plains. Camden was captured on February 22, 1922, when he showed back up at Thayer and was recognized by a Frisco brakeman who served as a deputy sheriff. The Oregon County sheriff happened to be in Thayer at the time and took charge of the prisoner. Accompanied by a private citizen, the sheriff started to Alton with his prisoner, but Camden, who was riding in the backseat, made a dash for freedom when the car slowed for a hill. The citizen and the sheriff gave chase on foot and recaptured Camden when "the prisoner's wind gave out" after about a quarter of a mile. Taken on to Alton, young Camden was charged only in the robbery of the Warren brothers, even though he had allegedly held up several other people in the Thayer area as well, including the Frisco brakeman who recognized him and arrested him. Camden was convicted in March and sent to the state penitentiary at Jefferson City for a five-year stretch. He was released early, however, on January 24, 1925, under the seven-twelfths "merit time" rule.

Camden's behavior while locked up might have been exemplary enough for him to gain an early release, but his prison time had apparently done little except turn him into a hardened criminal. Once on the outside, he quickly went on another crime binge, graduating to violence along the way.

Sometime around July 1, 1925, about five months after he had been released from Jeff City, Camden stopped at the home of his cousin, Burley Barton, near Oates, and invited Barton, younger brother of Enoch and Milton Barton, to go off with him. Barton, who was about three or four years younger than Camden, had never been away from home before, and he left against the protestations of his family.

The two young men promptly set out on a spree. At first, they committed a few burglaries and other petty crimes in their home territory of south-central Missouri, before ranging farther north into Pulaski and Miller counties. During the last week of July, they tried unsuccessfully to rob a bank at

Crocker, waylaid a citizen north of Crocker and forced him to write them a check, burglarized a home near Tuscumbia, and robbed another man at gunpoint southeast of Crocker. On or about August 1, they committed several depredations south of Waynesville. The sheriff of Pulaski County caught up with the two desperadoes and engaged them in a brief pistol battle but failed to capture either one.

The desperate duo wandered into Texas County and then Phelps County, "carrying out much the same plan that had been used to working the territory gone over."

About the fourth of August, Camden and Barton were spotted in southwestern Dent County at the Joy Post Office, where Barton shipped a suitcase to his family and mailed them a money order. As the pair continued to work their way east through southern Dent, the county sheriff, John R. Welch, received a tip that they were in the area and began trying to track them down. On the morning of August 5, Ernest Leonard, a farmer living near Stone Hill in eastern Dent County, discovered that the two fugitives had slept in his barn loft the night before, and he called the sheriff to report his finding. Sheriff Welch and Deputy George Redwine immediately set out for Stone Hill, where Leonard informed them that the two young hellions had started toward Howes Mill, about three miles east.

Joined by Leonard, Welch and Redwine started in pursuit of the fugitives and quickly overtook them at the foot of a nearby mound called Penrod Hill. Armed with a 45-70 Winchester rifle and standing on the running board of the posse's car, Welch ordered the pair to throw up their hands. Camden complied, but Barton started running and reached for a pistol he was carrying. Redwine fired four shots from his revolver at Barton, and Leonard also fired a shot, but the small-arms fire failed to halt the fleeing suspect. The deputy then shouted for Welch, who was still covering Camden, to shoot at Barton with his rifle.

The sheriff wheeled and fired a single shot that struck

the fleeing Barton in the back, stopping him in his tracks. He threw up his hands, fell to the ground, and died almost immediately.

In the meantime, as soon as Welch turned to fire at Barton, Camden seized the opportunity. Drawing a pistol, he fired at the sheriff and made a break for some nearby woods. Wounded slightly in the leg by Camden's gunshot, Welch got off two return shots but missed his target. His rifle jammed when he tried to fire a third shot, as Camden made his escape through a path in the woods that led to a nearby farmer's house.

Barton's body was taken to Salem to be prepared for burial. A note found on the body indicated that the two cousins expected to be killed at any time and asked that their parents be notified at their deaths.

The sheriff was also taken to Salem to have his wound treated, but another posse was hurriedly formed to go after the remaining fugitive. Officers of surrounding counties were notified to be on the lookout for Camden, and it was thought that he would be captured within a few hours. But after taking dinner at a home three miles east of where the gunfight had occurred and not far from his birthplace of Boss, the crafty Camden slipped the dragnet and made his way toward Arkansas.

On his trip south, Camden somehow picked up a traveling companion named Earl Ewell, a sixteen-year-old lad from Hannibal, Missouri. On August 26, the pair held up a crew at a gravel pit near Marked Tree, Arkansas, putting the Arkansas authorities on their trail. Officers caught up with them two days later, not far from the scene of the holdup, and another shootout ensued. During the gun battle, Camden was shot through the chest, with the bullet passing through his body just above the heart, while Ewell was captured without injury and placed in jail at nearby Harrisburg. The seriously wounded Camden was taken to a hospital in Memphis, Tennessee.

It was thought at first that his wound would prove fatal, but he eventually recovered and was sent to the Arkansas State Penitentiary in Little Rock in January of 1927.

Paroled after only a couple of years, Camden promptly went back to his criminal ways. In April of 1930, he spent a few days in the city jail in Wichita, Kansas, on an unknown charge, followed closely by a short stint in the Great Bend city jail.

Back in Missouri the following year, he hooked up with Mac Camden, another cousin, to carry out a string of burglaries in west-central Missouri. The pair were captured near Urbana in Hickory County on April 24 and brought back to St. Clair County to stand trial for a burglary committed a week earlier near the small community of Chloe. At their arraignment, Bobby Camden gave his name as Roy Coatch, and Mac Camden claimed he was Otis Parker. Convicted in late April of 1931 under their aliases, the two cousins were sentenced to four years in the state penitentiary and sent to Jefferson City before their true identities were discovered. Mac was paroled in November of 1932, while Bobby, presumably because of his prior offenses, was confined a while longer. He was discharged in June of 1933 when his sentence was conditionally commuted to time served.

This time, Camden waited an even shorter period than usual to resume his criminal career. He began almost immediately carrying out a string of burglaries and holdups in his home territory of south-central Missouri, including robbing the postmistress of the small community of Greeley, located in northwestern Reynolds County, on July 12, 1933, of fifteen dollars and fifty cents. (Ten days later, the Bank of Bunker, about five miles south of Greeley on the Reynolds-Dent county line, was held up by three men, but it's not known for sure whether Camden was one of the robbers.) Then on August 9, fifty-six-year-old James Radford, a well-known Reynolds County minister and farmer, was shot and killed from ambush in the barnyard of his home in the Marcoot neighborhood about five miles northwest of Greeley, and Camden was quickly named as a suspect in the case.

An intense manhunt ensued, and law officers from Reynolds County tracked Camden into Wayne County. They found him camped near Granite Bend on August 20 in the company of cousin Mac Camden; twenty-three-year-old Miss Allie Camden, another cousin; and nineteen-year-old Mrs. Bernice Radford, estranged wife of James Radford's nephew. With help from Wayne County lawmen, the officers surrounded the camp and fired on the party when Mac Camden reached for his gun. Mac Camden and the two women quickly surrendered and were taken into custody, but Robbie, as he was often called, bolted for the woods and escaped amid a hail of bullets fired by the officers.

During the next several months, as Camden continued to hide out in the hills eluding capture, his reputation took on a colorful, almost romantic, aspect, and his crimes seemed to become, at least to him, almost a lark. Proclaiming that he would never be taken alive, he sent "missives of defiance" to the sheriffs of Iron and Reynolds counties, and he reportedly issued an ultimatum outlawing hunting in Reynolds County, vowing that, if anyone approached him with a rifle cradled in his arms, he would kill the person on the spot. "It was reported," one newspaperman commented wryly, "fishing became a more popular sport."

As cold weather came on during the depression winter of 1933-34 and food became scarce, Camden supposedly issued another edict that no one in "his" territory should go hungry because he would provide. Thus was born the legend of the "Robin Hood of the Ozarks."

On the other hand, it was also reported that Camden "made the sale of padlocks . . . a booming business," as farmhouses were locked for the first time in memory, and he was not above resorting to the threat of violence to provide for his own needs. "His appearance . . . was the signal for farmers or their families to dig eagerly into larders to supply his wants," claimed one journalist. "He is said to have invited himself to dinners at the point of a pistol, superintending the meal's preparation, the housewife directing one fearful eye on his brandished pistol, the other on skillet and saucepan."

Camden was finally brought to bay in April of 1934 in the eastern edge of Dent County, just west of Bunker, by a small posse under Sheriff Malvern Jamison and Assessor Ray Brown of Reynolds County. Brown spotted the desperado heading toward the shelter of a cave and fired a rifle shot at him as Camden started to go for a pistol. The shot missed, but Camden, "concluding the assessor meant business," raised his hands and surrendered. Arriving on the scene almost immediately, the sheriff and his other deputies completed the arrest, taking two revolvers from the fugitive.

Taken to St. Louis for trial in the post-office robbery case, Camden was found guilty and sent back to Jefferson City under a thirty-year sentence in late May of 1934. Shortly afterward, perhaps deciding that he now had little to lose, Camden confessed to killing Reverend Radford at the behest of several other men. He said James Wofford, Wofford's son J. C. Wofford, and brothers Vernie and Emmet Smith had hired him to do the job, and Camden's uncle Will Camden and cousin Mac Camden were later implicated in the crime as well. Bobby Camden said the elder Wofford had promised him $200 to commit the murder but that he had received only $100. Camden said the motive of the men who hired him was that they blamed Radford for the death of his second wife, who was Vernie and Emmet Smith's mother. The woman had died in a car accident in which Radford was driving, but an inquest into the death had found no wrongdoing on Radford's part. However, according to Camden, the co-conspirators had called upon him to mete out their own brand of justice.

Camden's trial for the killing of Radford was scheduled for late May of 1936 in Reynolds County. Charges against Emmet Smith were dropped, but the trials of the other men on charges of conspiracy to commit murder were set to follow Camden's trial.

Newspaper photo of Robert Camden, 1936.

On May 27, Camden was brought to Reynolds County from Jefferson City under guard by the highway patrol. When he reached the county courthouse at Centerville, a crowd of hill folk was there to greet him. The eager onlookers included half a dozen female admirers who rushed up to him with kisses and embraces. Camden claimed not to know any of the women. During a brief recess of his trial, two young ladies sat on his lap and stroked his hair affectionately. "I can't see why the girls fall for an old codger like me," Camden remarked, "but I'm sure glad to get back and be with my girls."

Camden's trial ended abruptly when, during the midst of the proceeding, the defendant strode to the bench and announced that he wished to plead guilty. He declared that he didn't like the idea of going up against John H. Keith, a special prosecutor from Ironton, because "the rope was too plain" with Keith handling the case. Camden said he preferred to take his chances with the judge.

Before pronouncing sentence on the "tiny outlaw," as one report called Camden at the time, the judge immediately opened proceedings against James Wofford, whom Camden had accused of hiring him to kill Radford. Wofford testified in his own defense, claiming that Camden had invented the story to get even because he (Wofford) had laid a trap to help authorities capture Camden when the "undersized Ozarks bandit" was on the run after the killing. Wofford was found not guilty, and immediately afterward the judge sentenced Camden to life imprisonment. He was promptly returned to Jefferson City, only two days after he had left, to resume his now-extended prison term. (The cases of the other co-conspirators were postponed, but they, too, were presumably found not guilty.)

On April 28, 1951, Camden escaped from an auxiliary prison of the state penitentiary and came back to the hills of Reynolds County to hide out. He was recaptured less than three months later on July 19 at the home of his uncle, Cluster Black, near Centerville. He was armed with a 30-30 rifle when a sheriff's posse closed in on him, but he was captured before he had a chance to use it. Camden was taken to the Ironton jail and then on to Jefferson City, where, according to one newspaper report at the time, "he'll be just a number again."

Camden was discharged under parole on December 9, 1958, but the parole was revoked (for unknown reasons) less than a year later, and he was returned to the penitentiary on December 1, 1959. He was paroled again on May 3, 1966, and was finally freed altogether on April 26, 1971, when he was almost seventy years old. After his release, he returned once again to his familiar home territory and lived with family and friends until shortly before his death at the Arcadia Valley Hospital in Ironton on February 18, 1974.

Bibliography

Books and Articles

Barrow, Blanche Caldwell, and John Neal Phillips. *My Life with Bonnie and Clyde*. Norman: University of Oklahoma Press, 2004.

Brand, Peter. "Wyatt Earp, Jack Johnson, and the Notorious Blount Brothers." *Quarterly of the National Association for Outlaw and Lawman History* 27, no. 4 (October-December 2003).

Brown, Bizzy. "The Life and Times of Roscoe 'Red' Jackson." *White River Valley Historical Quarterly* 9, no. 1 (Fall 1985).

Cutler, William. *History of the State of Kansas*. Chicago: A. T. Andreas, 1883.

"The First White Settlers." *Journal of the Douglas County Historical and Genealogical Society, Inc.* (May 1987).

Gard, Wayne. *The Chisholm Trail*. Norman: University of Oklahoma Press, 1954.

Haase, Dixie. *The Hudson Family*. Printed by author, 2006.

Hartman, Mary, and Elmo Ingenthron. *Bald Knobbers: Vigilantes on the Ozarks Frontier*. Gretna, LA: Pelican, 1988.

Hegle, Jane Alsup. "Legendary James 'Shelt' Alsup and His Namesakes." *Journal of the Douglas County Historical and Genealogical Society, Inc.* (Summer 2007).

History of McDonald and Newton Counties. 1888. Reprint, McDonald County Historical Society, 1972.

Holcombe, R. I., ed. *History of Greene County, Missouri*. 1883. Reprint, Clinton, MO: Printery, 1969.

Hounschell, Jim. *Lawmen and Outlaws: 116 Years in Joplin History.* Marceline, MO: Walsworth, 1989.

Jenkins, Ernest. "The Fatal Horse Ride." *Journal of the Douglas County Historical and Genealogical Society, Inc.* (December 1989).

Lavender, David. *The Great West.* American Heritage, 1965.

Lederer, Katherine. "And Then They Sang a Sabbath Song." *Springfield Magazine* (April-June, 1981).

Livingston, Joel T. *A History of Jasper County and Its People.* Vol. 1. Chicago: Lewis, 1912.

Melton, Emory. "Double Murder and Lynching in White River Valley." *White River Valley Historical Quarterly* 4, no. 4 (Summer 1971).

Mitchell, John H. *Tales of the Bull Creek Country.* Cassville, MO: Litho, 1990.

Morgan, R. D. *The Tri-State Terror: The Life and Crimes of Wilbur Underhill.* Stillwater, OK: New Forums, 2005.

Palmquist, Robert F. "He Was about Half Way Right: Territory v Blount, 1881." *The Journal of Arizona History* (Winter 1999).

Paul, David. "Who Murdered Amanda Stevens?" *Arkansas Times* (October 1985): 102-8.

Phillips, John Neal. *Running with Bonnie and Clyde: The Ten Fast Years of Ralph Fults.* Norman: University of Oklahoma Press, 2002.

Stebbins, Chad. *All the News Is Fit to Print.* Columbia: University of Missouri Press, 1998.

Titsworth, Elizabeth. "The Last Hanging in Arkansas." *Wagon Wheels* 12, no. 1 (Spring 1992): 23-33.

War of the Rebellion: A Compilation of Official Records of the Union and Confederate Armies. 1880-1902. Reprint, Oakman, AL: H-Bar, 1996. CD-ROM.

Webb, Walter Prescott. *The Great Plains.* Boston: Ginn, 1959.

"Whoso Sheddeth Man's Blood, By Man Shall His Blood Be Shed." *White River Valley Historical Quarterly* 8, no. 12 (Summer 1985).

Zornow, William Frank. *Kansas: A History of the Jayhawk State.* Norman: University of Oklahoma Press, 1957.

Newspapers

Alton South Missourian-Democrat, various dates.

Batesville (AR) Guard, 13 November 1879.

Baxter Springs (KS) Cherokee Sentinel, 1868-71.

Baxter Springs Examiner, 1871.

Baxter Springs Herald, 1868.

Baxter Springs Sentinel, 1872.

Butler (MO) Bates County Record, December 1889.

Butler Democrat, December 1889.

Carthage Peoples Press, 25 January 1877.

Carthage (MO) Weekly Banner, various dates.

Columbus (KS) Workingman's Journal, 1869-72.

Crocker (MO) News, various dates.

Dardenelle (AR) Post Dispatch, 1913-14.

Ellington (MO) Press, various dates.

Flat River (MO) Lead Belt News, various dates.

Forsyth (MO) Taney County Republican, 1934.

Fort Scott Weekly Monitor, 25 January 1877.

Fort Smith Elevator, various dates.

Galena (KS) Miner, 23 June 1877 and 7 August 1879.

Galena (KS) Short Creek Republican, various dates.

Galena (MO) Stone County News Oracle, various dates.

Girard (KS) Weekly Press, 1870-72.

Granby (MO) Miner, various dates.

Houston (MO) Herald, 1906-7.

Ironton (MO) Iron County Register, various dates.

Joplin Daily Herald, various dates.

Joplin Globe, various dates.

Joplin Morning Herald, various dates.

Joplin News Herald, various dates.

Joplin Sunday Herald, various dates.

Kansas City Star, 21 and 22 February 1915.

Lamar (MO) Democrat, 1919.

Little Rock Arkansas Gazette, various dates.

Nashville (AR) News, 18 July 1914.

Neosho (MO) Miner and Mechanic, various dates.

Neosho Times, various dates.
New York Times, various dates.
Newtonia (MO) Newton County News, 1891.
Osceola (MO) St. Clair County Democrat, various dates.
Phoenix Arizona Gazette, 1885.
Phoenix Daily Herald, 1885.
Pierce City (MO) Weekly Empire, various dates.
Pleasant Hill (MO) Local, 26 February 1915.
Pleasant Hill Times, February-March 1915.
Poplar Bluff (MO) American Republican, various dates.
Rolla (MO) Weekly Herald, 15 June 1879.
Russellville (AR) Courier Democrat, 16 July 1914.
Salem (MO) News, various dates.
Springfield (MO) Daily News, 22 May 1937.
Springfield Express, various dates.
Springfield Leader and Press, various dates.
Springfield Leader Democrat, 29 November 1898.
Springfield Missouri Patriot, 9 and 16 December 1869.
Springfield Missouri Weekly Patriot, 13 and 20 March 1879.
Springfield Republican, various dates.
Union (MO) Franklin County Tribune, various dates.
Webb City (MO) New Century, 1877.
Yellville (AR) Mountain Echo, various dates.

Government Documents and Other Unpublished Sources
Alphabetical Commitment Register, Boonville State Training School for Boys, Missouri State Archives, Jefferson City.
Bates County Circuit Court Records.
Bishoff, Murray. Interview by author. 26 February 2001.
Blunt, Bud. Commutation file, Missouri State Archives, Jefferson City.
———. Pardon file, Missouri State Archives, Jefferson City.
———. Death certificate, Missouri State Archives Web site.
Britton, Lane. Extradition file, 1885, Arizona State Library, Archives and Public Records.
Childers, Linda. Interview by author. 9 March 2009.

Christian County Circuit Court Records, Christian County Library.

Clippings. "History of Baxter Springs." Baxter Springs Historical Museum, Baxter Springs, KS.

———. Johnston Public Library, Baxter Springs, KS.

Greene County Circuit Court Records, Greene County Archives and Records Center.

Jasper County Circuit Court Records, Jasper County Archives and Records Center.

Jasper County marriages, Jasper County Recorder's office.

Newton County Circuit Court Records, microfilm copies at Neosho/Newton County Library.

Pinkerton Agency Collection, Criminal Case Files, Box 71, Folder F, Library of Congress, Washington, D.C.

Register of Civil Proceedings, Missouri State Archives, Jefferson City.

Register of Escapes, Missouri State Penitentiary, Missouri State Archives, Jefferson City.

Register of Prisoners Received, Missouri State Penitentiary, Missouri State Archives, Jefferson City.

United States Census Records, various counties and census years.

Online Sources

"Albert Mansker: Last of the Arkansas Train Robbers." *The Mansker Chronicles.* www.mansker.org/history/albert.htm.

Armistead Family Tree. http://freepages.genealogy.rootsweb.ancestry.com/~jlbrown1820/Armistead%20Family%20Tree%201.html.

www.berea.edu/ENG/chestnut/lynching.html.

Brown, B. Gratz. Papers. "Missouri Digital Heritage." Missouri State Archives, Jefferson City. www.sos.mo.gov/archives.

http://ccharity.com.

Duff, Michael, and Barry Forman. "Hanged by the Neck Until Dead . . . Dead . . . Dead." *Bittersweet* 5, no. 3 (Spring 1978). http://thelibrary.springfield.missouri.org.

Emporia Daily Gazette, 6 March 1899. http://genforum. genealogy.com/cgi-bin/print.cgi?meadows::5642.html.

Fletcher (Parker), Sonja. "The Last Public Hanging in Arkansas." www.argenweb.net/logan/docsStevensMurder. html.

"History of the Jackson County Sheriff's Office." http:// jacksonsheriff.org/history.htm.

Liberty Tribune, 2 June 1871. "Missouri Digital Heritage." Missouri State Archives, Jefferson City. www.sos.mo.gov/ archives.

Luker, Lady Elizabeth. "The Olyphant Train Robbery." www. nhsalumni.net/newport/robbery.html.

Messages and Proclamations of the Governors of the State of Missouri. www.archive.org/stream/messagesandproc 1011925mbp/messagesandproc1011925mbp_djvu.txt.

"The Olyphant Train Robbery." *The Encyclopedia of Arkansas History and Culture*. www.encyclopediaofarkansas.net.

Phelps, John S. Papers. "Missouri Digital Heritage." Missouri State Archives, Jefferson City. www.sos.mo.gov/archives.

"Robert Camden: Robin Hood of the Ozarks." www. rootswebancestry.com/~mostfran/articles_crime/robert_ camden.htm.

www.rootsweb.ancestry.com/~mobarry/cemetery/old.carney/ old.carney.htm.

www.rootsweb.ancestry.com/~mobarry/data/news/ carneymurder.htm.

Saint Louis Globe Democrat, 17 March 1887. www. newspaperabstracts.com.

Soldiers' Records: War of 1812—World War I. "Missouri Digital Heritage." Missouri State Archives, Jefferson City. www.sos.mo.gov/archives.

Southwestern Reporter. Vol. 9, *Containing All the Current Decisions of the Supreme Courts of Missouri, Arkansas, and Tennessee; Court of Appeals of Kentucky; and Supreme Court and Courts of Appeal (Criminal Cases) of Texas, August 6, 1888-January 7, 1889.* St. Paul: West, 1889. Digitized by Google.

———. Vol. 56. *Decisions of the Supreme Courts of Missouri, April 23-June 11, 1900*. St. Paul: West, 1900. Digitized by Google.

———. *Containing All the Current Decisions of the Supreme and Appellate Courts of Arkansas, Kentucky, Missouri, Tennessee, and Texas, May 27-June 17, 1914*. St. Paul: West, 1914. Digitized by Google.

Springfield Press, 27 January 1933. Quoted at http://texashideout.tripod.com/reeds2.html.

"Tillman, John Arthur." *The Encyclopedia of Arkansas History and Culture*. www.encyclopediaofarkansas.net.

Index

Davis, Elizabeth, 46
Davis, G. G., 65-66
Decker, Al, 135
Delaware, Arkansas, 143-45, 147
Dent County, Missouri, 199, 202, 206
Denver, Colorado, 162
DeSoto, Missouri, 118
Dobbs, William T., 82, 86
Dockery, Alexander, 36
Doran, Alexander S., 77-78
Douglas County, Missouri, 44-51, 53-54
Doyle, Missouri, 200
Duncan, Horace, 128

Earp, Wyatt, 26, 33
Ellison, Dona, 191
Eoff, D. A., 87
Ewell, Earl, 203

Fagg, Alonzo, 79
Fagg, Elizabeth Tweedy, 74, 76
Fagg, Jack, 78
Fagg, James, 73, 78
Fagg, James H., 72
Fagg, Joel Pinkney, 72-74, 76-79
Fagg, Nettie, 79
Fagg, Pete, 78
Farrar, A. A., 171-72
Farris, Sam, 41
Fayetteville, Arkansas, 82-83, 88, 177-78
Fee, George, 186-87
Fisher, Billy, 148
Forsyth, Missouri, 191-93
Fort Scott, Kansas, 180-81, 186
Fort Smith, Arkansas, 77-79, 146, 177-78

Fowler, Laura, 134
Francisco, S. P., 91, 95
Frankfort, Kentucky, 189
Franklin County, Missouri, 116
Fuller, George, 186

Gainesville, Missouri, 194
Galena, Kansas, 40, 64, 126, 185, 189
Galena, Missouri, 131, 179, 193-96
Gardner, Frederick, 169-70
Gates, Elijah, 95
Gideon, J. R., 192
Gideon, Robert L., 193
Gillies, John, 34-35
Gilyard, Thomas, 127
Godley, French, 127
Godley, Montgomery, 131
Godley, Will, 126
Golden City, Missouri, 174, 176
Good, Thomas, 21-22
Goodykoontz, John, 40-41
Gowdy, Earl, 161, 163
Granby, Missouri, 27-29, 33-34, 37, 39-41, 43, 55-56, 60, 63-65
Greeley, Missouri, 204-5
Greene County, Missouri, 124-25, 173
Greenfield, Missouri, 174
Gunn, Joe, 179
Gwinn, S. L., 57

Hale, Hollis, 171-73
Hamilton, J. B. H., 138
Hamilton, Joseph, 132-42
Hamilton, Raymond, 178
Hampton, Pete, 127

222   DESPERADOES OF THE OZARKS